# BUILD A CYBER CITADEL

The No-Nonsense Guide to Cybersecurity for Startups & Small **Businesses**

**Copyright**

© Jonas Paul Dizon 2024

ISBN: 9798301668890

## Dedication

This book is dedicated to my amazing family:

To Gavin and Angelo, my tech-savvy teenage sons, whose bright minds and inquisitive spirits inspire me every day. May your futures be filled with success, happiness, and a passion for technology that drives positive change in the world.

And to my loving wife, Wivina, whose unwavering support, quick wit, infectious humor, and brilliant mind keep me grounded and motivated. Your love is my constant source of strength and inspiration.

## Personal Introduction

My journey in cybersecurity began in 1999 as a network and systems support specialist. Since then, I've had the privilege of working in diverse roles, spanning the spectrum of technology leadership: from independent software developer and project manager to IT operations manager and currently Senior Director of IT. This varied experience has given me a comprehensive understanding of the challenges businesses face in protecting their valuable assets from cyber threats.

Throughout my career, I've always been drawn to the transformative power of technology and its ability to drive innovation and growth. However, I've also witnessed firsthand the devastating consequences of cyberattacks, which can disrupt operations, damage reputations, and even threaten a company's survival. This has fueled my passion for helping businesses build robust cybersecurity defenses and cultivate a security-conscious culture.

While my current role as Senior Director of IT involves a broad range of responsibilities, I remain a key stakeholder in cybersecurity, recognizing its critical importance in today's interconnected world. In this book, I'll share my expertise and insights, gleaned from years of experience on the front lines of technology and security. Whether you're a seasoned IT professional or a non-technical business owner, this guide will equip you with the knowledge and tools you need to navigate the complex landscape of cybersecurity and safeguard your business from harm.

## Motivation for Writing the Book

I've noticed a significant gap in the cybersecurity landscape, not just within Canada, but globally. While large enterprises with dedicated security teams and extensive budgets have ample resources available, small and medium businesses (SMBs) worldwide often struggle to find concise, practical guidance tailored to their needs.

Many SMBs across the globe grapple with the complexities of cybersecurity, feeling overwhelmed by technical jargon, conflicting advice, and the misconception that they are "too small to be a target." This misconception can be dangerous, as cybercriminals increasingly prey on SMBs worldwide, recognizing them as vulnerable targets with potentially weaker defenses.

This book, *Build a Cyber Citadel*, is my attempt to bridge that gap and empower SMBs worldwide with the knowledge and tools they need to protect themselves. I've distilled my years of experience in various IT and cybersecurity roles into a clear and actionable guide, focusing on the essential elements of a robust cybersecurity program that can be applied globally.

My goal is to demystify cybersecurity, making it accessible and understandable for business owners and managers everywhere, regardless of their technical background. I want to provide them with the confidence and practical guidance they need to implement effective security measures, protect their valuable assets, and ensure the continued success of their businesses in the global marketplace.

## Target Audience

This book is written for you: the intrepid entrepreneurs, the visionary startup founders, the resilient small business owners, the IT managers ensuring smooth operations, and the bold managers who form the very foundation of the global economy.

You are the driving force behind innovation, the creators of jobs, the providers of essential services, and the dreamers who dare to challenge the status quo. You pour your heart and soul into building something meaningful, something that leaves a lasting impact on the world.

But in this era of relentless cyberattacks, your dedication and ingenuity need a shield—a cybersecurity shield forged in knowledge and vigilance.

Whether you're a tech-savvy innovator or someone who still grapples with the intricacies of the digital realm, this book is your guide. It's for those who recognize that cybersecurity is not merely an IT concern; it's a critical business imperative that can determine your success or failure in the face of relentless digital threats.

It's for those who are determined to protect their hard-earned data, their customers' trust, and their company's reputation from the ever-looming shadow of cybercrime. It's for those who understand that in this interconnected world, cybersecurity is not a luxury but an indispensable investment in the future of your business, your livelihood, and your dreams.

## Book Overview

In this book, I've distilled my 25+ years of experience in the IT trenches into a practical and accessible guide for SMBs. I'll take you on a journey through the essential elements of a robust cybersecurity program, demystifying complex concepts and empowering you to take control of your digital defenses.

We'll start by laying the foundation, exploring the core principles of cybersecurity and why they matter, even if you're "just a small business." You'll learn how to build a strong cybersecurity posture by implementing essential security measures, from crafting a clear cybersecurity policy to securing your endpoints, protecting your data, and fortifying your email and network infrastructure.

We'll then delve into the critical aspects of protecting your business operations, including navigating the cloud securely, managing employee access, and implementing a robust change management process. You'll also learn how to prepare for the unexpected with incident response and business continuity plans.

But cybersecurity is not just about technology; it's about people. We'll explore how to build a security-conscious culture within your organization, empowering your employees to become your first line of defense against cyber threats.

Finally, we'll examine the financial safety net of cybersecurity insurance, discussing its benefits, limitations, and how to choose the right policy for your business.

But our journey doesn't end there. In the final chapter, we'll explore the exciting and sometimes daunting world of Artificial Intelligence (AI) and its impact on cybersecurity. You'll learn about Large Language Models (LLMs) like ChatGPT, their potential benefits and risks, and how to integrate them safely into your business.

By the end of this book, you'll have a comprehensive understanding of cybersecurity and the practical steps you can take to protect your business from digital threats, both present and future. You'll gain the confidence and knowledge you need to navigate the ever-evolving cybersecurity landscape and ensure the continued success of your business in the digital age.

## Call to Action

The digital world is full of opportunities, but it's also fraught with risks. Don't let your business become another statistic. Take action today to protect your valuable assets, your customers' trust, and your hard-earned reputation.

This book, *Build a Cyber Citadel*, is your guide, your roadmap, and your toolkit for navigating the cybersecurity landscape. Use it wisely, implement the strategies, and build a security-conscious culture within your organization.

Remember, cybersecurity is not a destination; it's a journey. Stay vigilant, adapt to new threats, and continuously strengthen your defenses. The future of your business depends on it.

**Acknowledgements**

This book would not have been possible without the support and encouragement of many people.

I'd like to express my sincere gratitude to my family, especially my wife, for her unwavering support and patience throughout this writing process. Your love and encouragement kept me going. A special thanks to my Dad, whose sage advice has always kept me grounded and connected to the world around me.

I'm also grateful to my colleagues and mentors in the cybersecurity field who have shared their knowledge and insights over the years. Your expertise has been invaluable.

Finally, I'd like to thank you, the reader, for taking this journey with me. I hope this book empowers you to protect your business and thrive in the digital age.

**Connect with Me**

I'd love to connect with you and hear your thoughts on this book. You can find me on LinkedIn at the link below:

- LinkedIn: https://www.linkedin.com/in/jonaspaul/

# TABLE OF CONTENTS

# Chapter 1: Cybersecurity for Startups and Small Businesses: Why It Matters

Imagine this: It's Tuesday morning, and your small business is bustling. Orders are coming in, your team is busy, and everything seems to be running smoothly. Suddenly, your computers start displaying a menacing message: all your important files—customer records, financial data, product designs—are encrypted. A pop-up window demands a hefty ransom to unlock your systems and regain access to your critical data. Without those files, your operations grind to a halt. Orders can't be processed, invoices can't be generated, and employees can't do their jobs. This is the chilling reality of a ransomware attack, and it's a threat that looms over businesses of all sizes.

Small and medium businesses often believe they are too small to be targets, but this is a dangerous misconception. Cybercriminals are increasingly setting their sights on SMBs, recognizing them as "soft targets" with potentially weaker security measures. In fact, a 2023 study by the Canadian Federation of Independent Business (CFIB) found that nearly half of small businesses (45%) have experienced a random cyberattack in the past year, and 27% experienced a targeted attack.

These attacks can take many forms:

- **Data Breaches:** Think of all the sensitive information your business handles – customer names, addresses, credit card details, financial records, and maybe even confidential product designs or strategic plans. A data breach can expose this information to the world, leading to lawsuits, regulatory fines, and irreparable damage to your reputation.

- **Ransomware Attacks:** As you saw in our opening scenario, ransomware can bring your business to a screeching halt. Hackers encrypt your files and demand a ransom for the decryption key. Even if you pay the ransom, there's no guarantee you'll get your data back, and the downtime alone can be crippling.
- **Phishing Scams:** These are deceptive emails or messages designed to trick your employees into revealing sensitive information or downloading malware. One wrong click can compromise your entire network.
- **Denial-of-Service Attacks:** These attacks flood your website or online services with traffic, making them inaccessible to legitimate users. This can disrupt your operations, prevent customers from making purchases, and damage your brand's credibility.

Let me share a personal experience that really drove home the potential consequences of cyberattacks. A few years ago, I attended a security conference in Toronto where a speaker shared a chilling story about a hospital that had been hit with ransomware. Not only were their systems crippled, but the attack delayed critical surgeries and treatments, putting patients' lives at risk. This chilling example demonstrates how ruthless these cybercriminals can be and how attacks from the digital world can have severe consequences in the physical world, impacting the safety and well-being of real people.

## BUSTING CYBERSECURITY MYTHS

It's easy to fall into the trap of thinking "it won't happen to me," but cybersecurity threats are a real and present danger for businesses of all sizes. As Sun Tzu wisely stated in *The Art of War*, "If you know the enemy and know yourself, you need not fear the result of a hundred battles." Let's dispel some common myths that might be preventing you from truly knowing your enemy and securing your defenses:

- **Myth 1:** "We're too small to be a target." This is perhaps the most dangerous myth of all. Don't fall into the trap of "security by obscurity" – thinking that just because you're small, you'll fly under the radar. Cybercriminals often favor smaller businesses because they may have less robust security in place. They know that SMBs often have valuable data and may be easier to exploit than larger corporations with dedicated security teams.
- **Myth 2:** "We can't afford cybersecurity." Effective cybersecurity doesn't have to be expensive. There are many affordable solutions available, and the cost of preventing an attack is far less than the cost of recovering from one. Think of it as an investment in your business's future. A key principle here is Defense in Depth. This means implementing multiple layers of security so that even if one layer fails, others are there to protect you. It's like having a strong lock on your door, plus a security system, plus a watchful neighbor.
- **Myth 3:** "Cybersecurity is too complicated." You don't need to be a tech expert to protect your business. Implementing basic security measures, like those outlined in this book, can significantly reduce your risk. Start with the fundamentals and build from there.
- **Myth 4:** "I have antivirus software, so I'm protected." While antivirus is essential, it's only one piece of the puzzle. Cybersecurity is a multi-layered approach that includes strong passwords, secure configurations, employee training, and ongoing vigilance. This ties back into the idea of Defense in Depth – antivirus is just one layer of your overall defense strategy.

## THE COST OF DOING NOTHING

Ignoring cybersecurity is like leaving your front door wide open and hoping for the best. Sooner or later, someone is going to take advantage. In today's digital world, a cyberattack isn't a matter of *if* but *when*. The consequences can be severe, and they extend far beyond just financial loss:

- **Financial Impact:** Recovering from a cyberattack can feel like being caught in a financial whirlwind. Imagine this: Forensic investigators swarming your office, picking apart your systems to trace the attacker's every move. Lawyers huddled in your conference room, preparing for a potential class-action lawsuit from customers whose data was exposed. Your bank account draining as you pay for credit monitoring services, system repairs, and regulatory fines. And all the while, your sales screech to a halt as your website remains offline and your reputation lies in tatters.

- **Reputational Damage:** A cyberattack can shatter your company's hard-earned reputation overnight. It's like a digital scarlet letter emblazoned on your brand. Customers, once loyal, now eye your business with suspicion. Negative news articles and scathing online reviews spread like wildfire, eroding the trust you've spent years building. Winning back that trust can feel like climbing a mountain with a backpack full of rocks.

- **Operational Disruption:** A cyberattack can bring your business to a grinding halt. Picture this: arriving at your office to find your computers flashing a ransom note, your files encrypted, and your access denied. Your employees sit idle, unable to do their jobs. Phones ring unanswered, orders go unfulfilled, and frustration mounts. It's like your business has been hit by a digital hurricane, leaving chaos and uncertainty in its wake.

The statistics are sobering: According to a 2022 Statistics Canada survey, 21% of businesses reported being impacted by a cybersecurity incident. Of those businesses, 31% reported that the incident cost them between $100,000 and $500,000. But the true cost can be far greater when you factor in the intangible losses like reputational damage and lost opportunities. https://www150.statcan.gc.ca/n1/daily-quotidien/241021/dq241021a-eng.htm

Don't let your business become another statistic. Cybersecurity is not a luxury; it's a necessity in today's digital landscape. By taking proactive steps to protect your business, you can significantly reduce your risk and safeguard your hard-earned success. This book will guide you through the essential steps to build a strong cybersecurity foundation so you can face the digital world with confidence. Turn the page and let's get started!

# CHAPTER 2: YOUR CYBERSECURITY FOUNDATION: THE ESSENTIALS

Imagine building a Death Star. Would you start with the superlaser or the tractor beam? Of course not! You'd begin with a strong foundation to support everything else. Cybersecurity is no different. In this chapter, we'll lay the groundwork for a robust cybersecurity program by focusing on the essential elements that every small business needs. Even small steps can make a big difference in protecting your business from cyber threats, and prevent it from suffering a fate similar to Alderaan.

## CYBERSECURITY POLICY: YOUR GUIDING DOCUMENT

Think of a cybersecurity policy as the Bene Gesserit Litany Against Fear for your business when it comes to technology and data. (For those unfamiliar with the *Dune* universe, the Bene Gesserit are a powerful order who use a Litany Against Fear to overcome dangerous situations with a clear mind.) It's a written document that outlines your company's commitment to cybersecurity and provides clear guidelines for employees to follow. Even a basic policy can go a long way in preventing security breaches and establishing a culture of security awareness. "Fear is the mind-killer," as the saying goes in *Dune*. A strong cybersecurity policy helps your employees act with clarity and confidence, not fear, in the face of cyber threats.

## ENDPOINT PROTECTION: SECURING YOUR DEVICES

Your "endpoints" – your computers, laptops, smartphones, and any other device that connects to your network – are your first line of defense against cyberattacks. These devices are prime targets for cybercriminals, so securing them is critical.

Think of endpoint protection as equipping your business with the best armor and weaponry. Here's how to fortify your defenses:

- **Antivirus Software:** This is your digital shield, deflecting incoming attacks. Antivirus software scans your devices for malicious software (malware) and removes it before it can cause harm. Make sure to install reputable antivirus software on all your devices and keep it up to date.
- **Firewalls:** A firewall acts as a gatekeeper, controlling access to your network. It blocks unauthorized connections and prevents intruders from getting in. Ensure that your firewall is properly configured and enabled on all your devices.
- **Device Encryption:** Encryption scrambles your data, making it unreadable to anyone who doesn't have the decryption key. It's like having a secret code that only you can decipher. If your device is lost or stolen, encryption prevents thieves from accessing your sensitive information.
- **Software Updates:** Software updates often include security patches that fix vulnerabilities that attackers could exploit. Think of these updates as reinforcements that strengthen your defenses. Always keep your operating systems, applications, and other software up to date.

I've seen firsthand how the defense-in-depth mindset can be a lifesaver when it comes to endpoint protection. At a previous company, we had an employee lose their laptop—a situation that could have easily turned into a major data breach. But because we had implemented multiple layers of security, we were able to breathe a collective sigh of relief. We had strong password controls, the hard drive was encrypted with BitLocker, and we had the ability to remotely lock and wipe the device. Even though the physical device was lost, the sensitive data it contained remained protected. This experience solidified my belief in the power of a layered security approach.

## CHOOSING THE RIGHT ENDPOINT SOLUTION

Selecting the right endpoint solution is crucial for building a strong defense. Consider factors such as:

- **Features:** Look for a solution that offers comprehensive protection, including antivirus, anti-malware, intrusion detection, Data Loss Prevention, and firewall capabilities.
- **Ease of Use:** Choose a solution that is easy to deploy and manage, even if you don't have dedicated IT staff.
- **Compatibility:** Ensure the solution is compatible with your operating systems and devices.
- **Cost:** Evaluate the total cost of ownership, including licensing fees, maintenance, and support.

Some popular endpoint solutions for small businesses include Sophos Intercept X, SentinelOne, and Crowdstrike Falcon. These solutions offer a range of features and pricing options to suit different needs. Research and compare different options to find the best fit for your business.

## DATA PROTECTION: SAFEGUARDING YOUR CROWN JEWELS

In the digital age, data is the lifeblood of your business. Customer information, financial records, intellectual property – these are your crown jewels, and protecting them is paramount. A data breach can have devastating consequences, leading to financial loss, reputational damage, and legal liabilities.

Think of data protection as building a secure vault to safeguard your most valuable assets. Here's how to fortify your defenses:

- **Data Encryption:**
- Deep Dive: Encryption scrambles your data, making it unreadable to anyone who doesn't have the decryption key. Think of it like this: you have a safe with a complex combination lock. Only those who know the combination can open the safe and access its contents. Similarly, encryption

protects your data by transforming it into a jumbled mess that can only be deciphered with the correct key.

- o We'll focus on **encryption at rest**, which protects data stored on your devices. This is crucial because if a device is lost or stolen, the data on it is vulnerable to prying eyes.
- o One common method for encrypting data at rest is **full disk encryption (FDE)**. FDE encrypts the entire hard drive of a device, including the operating system and all user files. This means that even if someone removes the hard drive from your device and tries to access it from another computer, they won't be able to read the data without the decryption key.
- o **Illustrative Scenario**: Imagine you're a lawyer with a laptop full of sensitive client information. You use full disk encryption to protect this data. If your laptop is ever lost or stolen, you can rest assured that the thief won't be able to access your clients' confidential files.
- o **Types of Encryption at Rest**
  - When it comes to full disk encryption, there are a few common encryption algorithms:
  - **AES (Advanced Encryption Standard):** This is a widely used, robust encryption standard. It's considered very secure and is often the recommended choice for full disk encryption.
  - **XTS-AES:** This is a mode of operation for AES that is specifically designed for encrypting storage devices. It offers even stronger protection than standard AES.
  - **BitLocker:** BitLocker, the built-in encryption feature in Windows, typically uses XTS-AES.
- o **Recommended Encryption Type**
  - For most small businesses, **XTS-AES** is a solid choice for full disk encryption. It provides strong security and is readily available through tools like BitLocker or FileVault2 for MacOS. If you're using a cloud-based encryption management system, check what

encryption algorithms they support and follow their recommendations.

o **Deploying Company-Wide Disk Encryption**

o Protecting company data is paramount, and encrypting all company laptops is a crucial step. Here's a strategic approach to deploying disk encryption across your organization:

o **Choose the Right Solution:**

o Built-in Tools: Operating systems like Windows (BitLocker) and macOS (FileVault) offer built-in encryption tools. These can be effective for smaller organizations or those with basic needs.

o Cloud-Based Solutions: For larger organizations or those requiring centralized management, consider cloud-based encryption management systems. These offer features like remote encryption, key recovery, and compliance reporting.

o **Develop a Policy:**

o Create a clear policy outlining the requirements for laptop encryption. This policy should specify who is responsible for encryption, what types of devices are covered, and how encryption keys are managed.

o **Centralize Key Management:**

o Establish a secure system for managing encryption keys. This could involve using Active Directory, a cloud-based key management system, or a combination of both. Centralized key management ensures that you can recover data even if employees leave the company or lose their recovery keys.

o **Train Your Employees:**

o Educate employees about the importance of encryption and how to use it properly. Provide clear instructions on how to encrypt their laptops and what to do if they encounter any issues.

o **Monitor and Maintain:**

o Regularly monitor your encryption deployment to ensure that all laptops are encrypted and that policies are being followed. Keep your encryption software up to date to benefit from the latest security enhancements.

- o By following this strategic approach, you can effectively deploy disk encryption across your organization, safeguarding sensitive data and strengthening your overall security posture.

- **Access Controls:**
  - o Deep Dive: Not everyone needs access to the crown jewels. Access controls ensure that only authorized individuals can view, edit, or delete sensitive data. This involves implementing measures like:
    - Strong Passwords: Require employees to use strong, unique passwords and change them regularly.
    - Multi-Factor Authentication (MFA): Add another layer of protection by requiring users to provide multiple forms of authentication, such as requiring a one-time code sent to their phone or generated by a TOTP app, on top of a strong password.
    - Role-Based Access Control (RBAC): Assign permissions based on job roles, ensuring that employees only have access to the data they need to perform their duties.
  - o Illustrative Scenario: A healthcare provider uses RBAC to ensure that only doctors and nurses can access patient medical records, while administrative staff have access to billing information but not sensitive medical data. Having a MFA implemented ensures that even if their passwords ever get leaked, the additional authentication factors will keep hackers from being able to use their user accounts.

- **Secure Data Storage and Backup:**
  - o Deep Dive: Where you store your data matters. Choose secure storage solutions, whether on-site or in the cloud. Implement regular backups to protect against data loss due to hardware failure, accidental deletion, or ransomware attacks.

- On-site storage: If you store data on-site, use secure servers with access controls and environmental protections (e.g., fire suppression, temperature control).
- Cloud storage: If you use cloud storage, choose reputable providers with strong security measures and compliance certifications (e.g., ISO 27001, SOC 2).
- Backups: Follow the 3-2-1 backup rule: keep at least three copies of your data, on two different media types, with one copy stored off-site.
  - Illustrative Scenario: A law firm backs up its sensitive client data daily to both an on-site server and a secure cloud storage service. This ensures they can recover their data even if their office is damaged by a fire or flood.

- **Data Disposal and Sanitization:**
  - Deep Dive: When you dispose of old devices or data, ensure it's done securely to prevent data breaches. Methods include:
    - Wiping Hard Drives: Use software to completely erase data from hard drives before disposing of or reusing them.
    - Physical Destruction: For highly sensitive data, consider physical destruction of hard drives (e.g., shredding, degaussing).
    - Secure Document Shredding: Shred paper documents containing sensitive information.
    - You can use data destruction service providers that can issue destruction certificates for each hard drive or storage device that they destroy.
  - Illustrative Scenario: A bank securely wipes the hard drives of all its old computers before donating them to a local school, ensuring that no customer financial data is left behind.

- **Data Loss Prevention (DLP):**

o Deep Dive: DLP tools and techniques act as your data guardians, monitoring and controlling the flow of sensitive information. They can:
- Identify Sensitive Data: Classify data based on its sensitivity (e.g., confidential, restricted, public).
- Monitor Data Movement: Track how data is being accessed, used, and shared.
- Prevent Unauthorized Access and Sharing: Block or quarantine attempts to send sensitive data outside the organization or to unauthorized individuals.
- Enforce Data Handling Policies: Ensure that employees follow company policies for handling sensitive information.

o Illustrative Scenario: A company uses DLP software to prevent employees from emailing sensitive customer data to their personal email accounts or uploading it to unauthorized cloud storage services.

## EMAIL PROTECTION: DON'T GET HOOKED BY PHISHING

Email is the digital equivalent of your company's front door. It's how you communicate with customers, partners, and employees. But just like a physical door, it can also be an entry point for unwanted visitors – cybercriminals who use email to deliver malicious payloads, steal sensitive information, and wreak havoc on your business.

Think of email protection as installing a security system for your digital front door. It involves implementing measures to prevent unauthorized access, detect suspicious activity, and protect your business from email-borne threats.

Here's how to fortify your email defenses:

- **Employee Training and Awareness:**

- o **Recognize Phishing:** Train employees to recognize and avoid phishing emails – deceptive messages designed to trick them into revealing sensitive information (like passwords or credit card numbers) or downloading malware. Teach them to:
  - Be wary of suspicious sender addresses or links.
  - Hover over links to see the actual destination before clicking.
  - Never open attachments from unknown senders.
  - Report suspicious emails to the IT department or security team.
- o **Email Security Best Practices:** Educate employees on email security best practices, such as:
  - Using strong, unique passwords for email accounts.
  - Enabling multi-factor authentication (MFA) for added security.
  - Avoiding sending sensitive information via email whenever possible.
  - Using a digital signature to verify the authenticity of emails.
- o **Pro Tip: Phishing Tests:** Conduct regular phishing tests to assess employee awareness and reinforce training. These tests involve sending simulated phishing emails to employees to see if they fall for the bait. If they do, provide additional training and guidance. Several companies offer phishing testing platforms, including KnowBe4, and Proofpoint Security Awareness Training.
- o **Personal Tip:** In today's mobile world, many employees access their work email on their smartphones. However, due to the smaller screen size and simplified user interface, it can be more challenging to spot phishing emails on mobile devices. That's why it's crucial to train your employees on how to recognize phishing attempts,

regardless of the device they're using. Furthermore, consider configuring your email server to block emails that fail SPF (Sender Policy Framework) checks. This adds an extra layer of protection against spoofing attacks and helps prevent phishing emails from reaching your employees' inboxes in the first place.

- **Spam Filters:**
  - ○ Spam filters are like the gatekeepers of your inbox, blocking unwanted and potentially harmful emails before they reach your employees. Most email providers offer built-in spam filters, but you can also implement additional filtering solutions for enhanced protection.
- **Email Authentication Protocols:**
  - ○ Email authentication protocols like SPF (Sender Policy Framework), DKIM (DomainKeys Identified Mail), and DMARC (Domain-based Message Authentication, Reporting & Conformance) help validate the authenticity of emails, making it more difficult for spammers and phishers to spoof your domain.
- **Anti-Malware Scanning:**
  - ○ Implement anti-malware scanning for all incoming and outgoing emails to detect and block malicious attachments or links.

## ACCESS CONTROLS: GUARDING THE GATES

Imagine your company's sensitive data as a castle. You wouldn't leave the gates wide open for anyone to wander in, would you? Access controls are like the guards at your castle gates, ensuring that only authorized individuals can enter and access specific areas.

In the digital realm, access controls determine who can view, edit, or delete sensitive data. This involves implementing measures like:

- **Strong Passwords:** Think of passwords as the first line of defense at your castle gates. Strong passwords are like sturdy locks, making it difficult for unauthorized users to break in. Require employees to use strong, unique passwords for all their accounts and change them regularly. A strong password should be:

- o Lengthy: At least 12 characters long.
- o Complex: Include a mix of uppercase and lowercase letters, numbers, and symbols.
- o Unique: Don't reuse passwords across different accounts.
- o Random: Avoid using easily guessable words or patterns.
- o Pro Tip: Consider using a passphrase instead of a single word. A passphrase is a longer, memorable phrase that's easier to remember but still difficult to crack. For example, "MyPetRockCantPlayFetch" is a strong passphrase.

- **Multi-Factor Authentication (MFA):** MFA adds an extra layer of security, like having a second guard at the gate who demands additional identification. Even if someone manages to steal or guess a password, they won't be able to access the account without the second factor, such as a one-time code sent to their phone or a fingerprint scan.
  - o Implementation Tip: Many online services and applications offer MFA options. Encourage employees to enable MFA wherever possible, especially for critical accounts like email, banking, and social media.
  - o The Future is Passwordless: While passwords remain prevalent, the industry is gradually shifting towards passwordless authentication methods. This eliminates the risks associated with password theft, reuse, and phishing attacks. Instead of relying on something you know (a password), passwordless authentication uses something you have (a physical key or device) or something you are (biometric data).
  - o How Passwordless Authentication Works:
    - Passkeys: These are digital keys stored securely on your device or in a password

manager. When you try to log in to a website or app, you'll receive a prompt on your device to verify your identity, often using biometrics like fingerprint scanning or facial recognition.

- Security Keys: Physical security keys, like YubiKeys, plug into your device's USB port or connect wirelessly. They generate unique codes that are used to authenticate your identity.
- Biometrics: Biometric authentication uses your unique physical characteristics, such as fingerprints, facial features, or iris patterns, to verify your identity. Many devices now have built-in biometric sensors for this purpose.

- Added Insight: Implementing MFA is crucial in today's world of frequent data breaches and password leaks. Let's face it, despite our best efforts to educate users about password hygiene, many people still reuse passwords across multiple accounts. And when those personal accounts get compromised, hackers can easily try those same credentials on work accounts. MFA acts as a powerful deterrent in these situations, stopping those attacks in their tracks even if the password has been leaked.

- **Role-Based Access Control (RBAC):** RBAC is like assigning different keys to different people based on their roles in the castle. It ensures that employees only have access to the data they need to perform their duties. For example, a marketing team member might have access to marketing data but not financial records, while a finance team member would have the opposite permissions.

  - Best Practice: Regularly review user permissions and access rights to ensure they are still appropriate. When employees change roles or leave the company, promptly revoke their access to sensitive data.

**Illustrative Scenario:**

Picture this: You're the owner of a busy dental practice. Patient records, billing information, and employee data are all stored digitally. To protect this sensitive information, you've implemented a robust access control system.

First, you require all employees to use strong, unique passwords and enable MFA on their accounts. This ensures that even if a password is compromised, unauthorized access is still blocked.

Next, you implement RBAC. Your receptionists can access appointment schedules and patient contact information but not medical records. Hygienists can access patient dental charts but not billing information. And only you and your office manager have access to all data, including financial records and employee information.

This layered approach gives you peace of mind knowing that your patients' data is secure, and your practice is protected from potential breaches.

**Key Takeaways:**

- Access controls are essential for protecting sensitive data and preventing unauthorized access.
- Implement strong passwords, MFA, and RBAC to create a layered defense.
- Regularly review and update user permissions to ensure they are still appropriate.

CONFIGURATION MANAGEMENT: SECURING YOUR SYSTEMS

Think of your computer systems and software as a newly built house. Before you move in, you'd want to make sure all the doors and windows are locked, the alarm system is activated, and any potential hazards are secured. Configuration management is like that pre-move-in security check for your technology.

It involves setting up your operating systems, applications, and network devices in a secure way to minimize vulnerabilities and protect against cyberattacks. It's about making sure the "default" settings are secure and that any unnecessary features or services are disabled.

Here's why configuration management matters:

- Reduces Attack Surface: Secure configuration minimizes the ways attackers can exploit your systems. It's like locking down all the potential entry points to your digital house.
- Prevents Misconfigurations: Many cyberattacks exploit misconfigured systems. Configuration management helps prevent these errors and ensures a consistent security baseline.
- Improves Compliance: Secure configuration is often a requirement for compliance with industry standards and regulations (e.g., PCI DSS, HIPAA).

**Key Configuration Management Practices:**

- Use Secure Defaults: When installing software or setting up devices, choose the most secure default settings. This might involve enabling firewalls, disabling unnecessary services, and setting strong password policies.
- Principle of Least Privilege: Configure systems to grant users only the minimum necessary access to perform their tasks. This limits the potential damage if an account is compromised.
- Regular Updates and Patching: Keep your software up to date with the latest security patches. This fixes known vulnerabilities and protects against emerging threats.
- Configuration Monitoring: Regularly monitor your systems' configurations to ensure they haven't been tampered with or misconfigured.

ESTABLISHING A SECURITY BASELINE

A security baseline is a set of standardized security configurations that should be applied to all your devices and systems. This ensures a consistent level of security across your organization and helps prevent common vulnerabilities.

**Important Note:** A security baseline is not a static document. It needs to be reviewed and updated periodically, at least annually, to ensure it still aligns with your organization's security posture and industry best practices. As your business grows, technology evolves, and new threats emerge, your security baseline must adapt to maintain its effectiveness.

Here are some examples of settings you might include in your security baseline:

- Firewall: Ensure the firewall is turned on for all devices, blocking unauthorized network connections.
- Disk Encryption: Encrypt all hard drives to protect data in case of device loss or theft.
- Screen Lock Timeout: Set a short screen lock timeout (e.g., 5 minutes) to prevent unauthorized access to unattended devices.
- Password Complexity: Enforce strong password policies, requiring a minimum length, complexity, and regular password changes.
- Antivirus Software: Install and maintain up-to-date antivirus software on all devices.
- Software Updates: Configure automatic updates for operating systems and applications to ensure timely patching of security vulnerabilities.

## Tools for Endpoint Configuration Management

Managing the configurations of numerous endpoint computers can be a complex task. Fortunately, various tools are available to streamline and automate this process:

- Microsoft Intune: A cloud-based service that allows you to manage and secure Windows, macOS, Android, and iOS devices. It provides features for configuration management, software deployment, and security policy enforcement.

- Jamf Pro: A comprehensive management solution for Apple devices, offering configuration management, app distribution, and security controls.
- ManageEngine Endpoint Central: A unified endpoint management platform that supports Windows, macOS, and Linux. It provides features for configuration management, patch management, and software deployment.

These tools can help you ensure that your endpoint computers are configured securely and consistently, reducing your attack surface and improving your overall security posture.

**Illustrative Scenario:**

Imagine you're setting up a new Wi-Fi network for your office. Secure configuration is crucial to prevent unauthorized access. Here are some key steps:

- Change Default Passwords: Change the default administrator password for your Wi-Fi router to a strong, unique password.
- Enable Network Encryption: Use WPA2 or WPA3 encryption to protect your Wi-Fi traffic from eavesdropping.
- Disable WPS: WPS (Wi-Fi Protected Setup) can be vulnerable to attacks. Disable it if possible.
- Enable Firewall: Ensure the firewall on your router is enabled to block unauthorized connections.
- Regularly Update Firmware: Keep your router's firmware up to date to patch security vulnerabilities.

By following these configuration management practices, including using appropriate tools and establishing a security baseline, you can significantly strengthen your security posture and reduce the risk of cyberattacks.

**Concluding Remarks**

Building a strong cybersecurity foundation is like constructing a well-defended Cyber Citadel. By implementing the essential elements we've covered in this chapter – from establishing a clear cybersecurity policy to securing your endpoints and data – you create a resilient defense against cyber threats.

As Sun Tzu wisely stated in *The Art of War*, "The supreme art of war is to subdue the enemy without fighting." By proactively strengthening your cybersecurity posture, you deter attackers and reduce the likelihood of a costly battle.

Remember, cybersecurity is not a one-time event; it's an ongoing process of vigilance and adaptation. Continuously assess your defenses, stay informed about emerging threats, and refine your strategies to stay ahead of the curve.

Now that you've laid the foundation, let's move on to Chapter 3, where we'll explore how to protect your business operations from specific cyber threats.

## CHAPTER 3: PROTECTING YOUR BUSINESS OPERATIONS

Imagine your business as a bustling marketplace. You have merchants selling their wares, customers browsing the stalls, and goods flowing in and out. But what if thieves were lurking in the shadows, looking for opportunities to steal valuables or disrupt the flow of commerce?

Cybersecurity is not just about protecting your technology; it's about safeguarding your business operations from those digital thieves. It's about ensuring that your marketplace runs smoothly, securely, and efficiently, even in the face of cyber threats.

In this chapter, we'll explore key areas of operational security, equipping you with the knowledge and tools to protect your business from disruption, data breaches, and financial loss.

We'll start by navigating the cloud securely, ensuring your business can reap the benefits of cloud computing without exposing itself to unnecessary risks. Then, we'll delve into the critical processes of employee onboarding and offboarding, ensuring secure transitions and minimizing vulnerabilities. Finally, we'll explore the importance of change management, guiding you on how to implement changes safely and avoid introducing security gaps.

By the end of this chapter, you'll have a solid understanding of how to protect your business operations from cyber threats, ensuring your digital marketplace thrives in a secure and resilient environment.

## CLOUD COMPUTING: SCALING NEW HEIGHTS, SECURELY

The cloud has revolutionized how businesses operate, offering scalability, flexibility, and cost-effectiveness. But like any new frontier, it comes with its own set of challenges, particularly when it comes to security.

Think of the cloud as a vast digital landscape, with towering servers, sprawling data centers, and endless connections. It's a powerful resource, but it's also a shared space, with potential risks lurking around every corner.

In this section, we'll guide you through the essentials of cloud security, ensuring your business can harness the power of the cloud while minimizing its risks.

### Choosing a Secure Cloud Provider

Selecting the right cloud provider is the first step towards secure cloud computing. It's like choosing a trustworthy guide for your journey through the digital landscape. Here are some key factors to consider:

- Security Certifications: Look for providers with recognized security certifications, such as ISO 27001 (information security management) and SOC 2 (security, availability, processing integrity, confidentiality, and privacy). These certifications demonstrate that the provider has met rigorous security standards.

- Data Encryption: Ensure the provider uses strong encryption to protect your data both in transit (when it's moving between your devices and the cloud) and at rest (when it's stored on their servers).
- Access Controls: Understand the provider's access control policies. How do they authenticate users and authorize access to data? Do they offer features like multi-factor authentication and role-based access control?
- Data Storage Location: Consider where your data will be stored. Does the provider's data center location comply with relevant data privacy regulations (e.g., GDPR, CCPA)?
- Compliance: If your business operates in a regulated industry (e.g., healthcare, finance), ensure the provider complies with relevant regulations (e.g., HIPAA, PCI DSS).

**Securing Your Cloud Data and Applications: Building a Fortress in the Digital Sky**

Choosing a secure cloud provider is just the first step. Once you've entrusted your data and applications to the cloud, it's crucial to take proactive steps to protect them. Think of it as building a fortress in the sky, fortifying your digital assets against potential threats.

But first, let's clarify what we mean by "the cloud." In this context, we're primarily referring to cloud-based applications and services that you use to run your business, such as email, file storage, customer relationship management (CRM), and productivity suites. These fall under the category of Software as a Service (SaaS).

Here's a quick overview of the different types of cloud services:

- Infrastructure as a Service (IaaS): This provides access to fundamental computing resources like servers, storage, and networking. You manage the operating systems and applications yourself. Examples include Amazon Web Services (AWS), Microsoft Azure, and Google Cloud Platform (GCP).
- Platform as a Service (PaaS): This provides a platform for developing and deploying applications, including the

underlying infrastructure and operating systems. You manage the applications themselves. Examples include Heroku, AWS Elastic Beanstalk, and Google App Engine.

- Software as a Service (SaaS): This provides access to software applications over the internet. You don't manage the infrastructure or the application itself; you simply use the software. Examples include Google Workspace, Microsoft Office 365, Salesforce, and Dropbox.

While the security principles we'll discuss apply broadly to all types of cloud services, our focus in this section is primarily on SaaS, as these are the most commonly used cloud services by small and medium businesses.

## ESSENTIAL SECURITY MEASURES FOR SAAS

Here are some essential security measures to implement when using SaaS applications:

- **Strong Passwords and MFA:** Use strong, unique passwords for all your cloud accounts and enable multi-factor authentication wherever possible. This adds an extra layer of defense against unauthorized access.
- **Access Controls:** Configure access controls carefully, granting users only the necessary permissions to perform their tasks. Regularly review and update user permissions as needed.
- **Encryption:** Encrypt sensitive data before storing it in the cloud. This adds an extra layer of protection in case of a data breach.
- **Regular Monitoring:** Monitor your cloud activity for suspicious behavior, such as unusual login attempts or data access patterns. Many cloud providers offer security monitoring tools and alerts.
- **Data Backup and Recovery:** Even with the best security measures in place, data loss can still occur due to accidental deletion, hardware failure, or ransomware attacks. Regularly back up your cloud data to a separate location, preferably

another cloud provider or an on-premises server. Ensure you have a robust data recovery plan to restore your data quickly in case of an incident.

- **Secure Configuration:** Just as you would secure your physical office with locks, alarms, and security cameras, secure your cloud environment with proper configuration. Follow security best practices for configuring your cloud services, such as disabling unnecessary features, enabling firewalls, and implementing intrusion detection systems. Regularly review and update your cloud configurations to ensure they align with your security policies and industry best practices.

## EMPLOYEE ONBOARDING/OFFBOARDING: SECURE TRANSITIONS

Think of your employees as members of your company's crew, sailing together on the ship of business. When new crew members come aboard, they need proper training and guidance to navigate the ship safely and efficiently. And when crew members depart, it's crucial to ensure a smooth handover and prevent them from taking any valuable cargo with them.

Employee onboarding and offboarding are like the embarkation and disembarkation processes for your digital ship. They involve managing user access, providing security awareness training, and securing company assets during employee transitions.

Here's how to ensure secure and efficient onboarding and offboarding:

**Onboarding: Welcoming New Crew Members**

- **Grant Appropriate Access:** Provide new employees with access to only the systems and data they need to perform their job duties. Avoid granting excessive permissions that could lead to security risks.
- **Security Awareness Training:** Incorporate security awareness training into the onboarding process. Educate

new employees about company security policies, password guidelines, data protection procedures, and how to recognize and avoid phishing scams.

- **Set the Tone:** Emphasize the importance of cybersecurity from day one, establishing a culture of security awareness and responsibility.

## Offboarding: Bidding Farewell Securely (and Amicably)

When an employee leaves the company, it's crucial to handle the offboarding process securely and professionally. A negative offboarding experience can increase the risk of insider threats, data breaches, and even sabotage.

- **Why a Friendly Offboarding Matters:**
  - **Reduced Risk:** Studies show that employees who have a negative offboarding experience are more likely to engage in risky behavior, such as stealing data or disrupting systems. A 2021 survey by Osterman Research found that 70% of organizations had experienced data theft by departing employees.
  - **Reputation Protection:** A smooth offboarding process helps maintain a positive company reputation and reduces the likelihood of legal issues or negative publicity.
  - **Knowledge Transfer:** A friendly offboarding facilitates knowledge transfer and ensures a smooth transition for remaining employees.
- **Key Steps for Secure Offboarding:**
  - **Revoke Access:** Promptly revoke access to all company systems and data upon the employee's departure. This prevents former employees from accessing sensitive information or causing harm.
  - **Secure Company Devices:** Retrieve company laptops, mobile devices, and any other company property. Ensure that data is securely wiped from these devices before they are reassigned or disposed of.

- o **Exit Interviews:** Conduct exit interviews to remind departing employees of their confidentiality obligations and to collect any company-owned data or devices they may still possess. Use this opportunity to understand their experience and gather feedback. * **Offer Outplacement Services:** Consider providing outplacement services to departing employees, especially those who may need assistance with their job search. This can include career counseling, resume writing assistance, interview preparation, and access to job boards. Partnering with organizations that specialize in outplacement services can streamline this process. * **Maintain Professionalism:** Treat departing employees with respect and dignity, even in difficult situations. This helps minimize resentment and reduces the risk of retaliatory actions.

## CHANGE MANAGEMENT: NAVIGATING CHANGE SAFELY

In the dynamic world of business, change is inevitable. New software is implemented, systems are upgraded, and configurations are adjusted to meet evolving needs. However, even seemingly small IT changes can have unintended consequences, introducing security vulnerabilities or disrupting critical operations.

Think of change management as the navigation system for your business's IT journey. It helps you chart a safe and efficient course through the ever-changing technology landscape, ensuring that changes are implemented smoothly and securely.

I recall an experience where I helped a small software company stabilize their production environment. They were experiencing frequent outages and instability, and it was a real struggle to pinpoint the root cause. It turned out that their developers had direct access to the production servers, and there was no process for code review or change approvals. Essentially, they had no proper change management process. To address this, we introduced a change management process with preventative controls. We removed the developers' direct access to the servers and applications and implemented a mandatory peer code review and QA process before any changes could be deployed. This brought much-needed stability to their production environment and significantly reduced the number of incidents.

Here's how to implement a secure change management process:

- **Document All Changes:** Keep a detailed record of all planned and implemented changes, including the reasons for the change, the systems affected, and the individuals involved. This documentation provides a valuable audit trail and helps with troubleshooting if problems arise.
- **Implementation Tip: Use a Wiki:** Consider using a wiki-style platform for documentation. This allows employees to easily access, create, and modify information, fostering collaboration and ensuring everyone has access to the latest updates. Popular wiki platforms include Atlassian Confluence, Notion, and Microsoft Teams wiki functionality.
- **Test in a Controlled Environment:** Before deploying changes to production systems, test them thoroughly in a controlled environment, such as a staging or development environment. This allows you to identify and address any issues before they impact your live systems.
- **Have a Rollback Plan:** In case a change introduces unexpected problems or vulnerabilities, have a rollback plan to revert to the previous configuration. This minimizes downtime and reduces the impact on your business operations.
- **Communicate Effectively:** Communicate planned changes to affected employees and stakeholders, providing clear explanations and timelines. This helps manage expectations and ensures everyone is prepared for the change.
- **Monitor After Implementation:** After implementing a change, monitor your systems closely for any unexpected behavior or performance issues. This helps identify and address any unforeseen problems quickly.

- **Establish an Approval Process:** Implement a clear approval process for all changes, ensuring that changes are authorized by appropriate personnel and prioritized based on their potential impact and urgency. This helps prevent unauthorized changes and ensures that critical systems are not disrupted.

## INCIDENT RESPONSE AND BUSINESS CONTINUITY: WEATHERING THE STORM

Imagine a sudden storm hitting your business. Rain is pouring in through a broken window, the power goes out, and your customers are stranded. How would you react? A well-prepared business would have a plan to secure the building, restore essential services, and communicate with customers.

Cybersecurity incidents and other disruptions are like those unexpected storms. They can strike at any time, causing damage, disrupting operations, and threatening your business's survival. That's where incident response and business continuity plans come in.

### Incident Response: Your Emergency Action Plan

An incident response plan is like a fire drill for your digital world. It outlines the steps to take in case of a cybersecurity incident, such as a data breach, ransomware attack, or denial-of-service attack. A well-defined plan helps you:

- React Quickly: Minimize the damage by taking swift action to contain the incident.
- Coordinate Efforts: Ensure everyone knows their roles and responsibilities.
- Communicate Effectively: Inform stakeholders and provide updates.
- Recover Efficiently: Restore systems and data to resume normal operations.

**Key Components of an Incident Response Plan:**

- Incident Identification: Establish clear criteria for identifying and classifying security incidents.
- Containment: Outline steps to isolate affected systems and prevent further damage.
- Eradication: Detail how to remove the threat, such as malware or unauthorized access.
- Recovery: Describe the process for restoring data and systems to their pre-incident state.
- Lessons Learned: Include a process for analyzing the incident, identifying root causes, and improving your security posture.

**Business Continuity: Keeping the Lights On**

A business continuity plan is like having a backup power generator. It ensures that your business can continue operating even during a major disruption, such as a natural disaster, power outage, or cyberattack. A solid plan helps you:

- Identify Critical Functions: Determine the essential functions that must continue operating during a disruption.
- Develop Recovery Strategies: Outline how to restore those critical functions, including alternative work locations, backup systems, and communication plans.
- Minimize Downtime: Reduce the impact on your business operations and customers.

**Tabletop Exercises: Practicing for the Storm**

Tabletop exercises are simulations that allow your team to practice their response to various scenarios. They are like fire drills for your incident response and business continuity plans. During a tabletop exercise, your team will:

- Gather in a room and work through a hypothetical scenario, such as a ransomware attack or a data breach.

- Discuss their roles and responsibilities, make decisions, and test their communication and coordination.
- Identify gaps in their plans and improve their preparedness.

## Making Tabletop Exercises Fun and Engaging

While tabletop exercises address serious topics, they don't have to be dull and dry. In fact, making them engaging and even a bit fun can increase participation, improve learning, and foster a stronger security culture.

- Gamification: Introduce game-like elements, such as points, rewards, or friendly competition, to make the exercise more interactive and motivating.
- Real-World Scenarios: Use realistic scenarios that resonate with your team and reflect potential threats to your specific industry or business.
- Interactive Elements: Incorporate interactive elements, such as role-playing, simulations, or multimedia presentations, to keep participants engaged.
- Debriefing and Feedback: Conclude the exercise with a debriefing session where participants can share their observations, feedback, and suggestions for improvement.

## Why Annual Exercises are Key

Running tabletop exercises annually is crucial for maintaining a state of preparedness. This allows you to:

- Refresh your team's knowledge and skills.
- Incorporate lessons learned from previous exercises or real-world incidents.
- Adapt your plans to address new threats and vulnerabilities.
- Ensure your team is ready to respond effectively in case of a real emergency.

The Power of Preparation: I've seen firsthand the value of business continuity planning in navigating unexpected disruptions. In 2018, my organization conducted a tabletop exercise where we simulated our office burning down, rendering it unusable and forcing employees to work remotely. This was before the pandemic, when remote work wasn't the norm. The exercise revealed some gaps in our ability to support a remote workforce. As a result, we invested in laptops for everyone, moved our phone systems to the cloud, implemented Zero Trust VPNs, and tested the viability of everyone working from home. Then, when the COVID-19 pandemic hit in 2020, our transition to remote work was seamless! While other companies scrambled to adapt, we were well-prepared, thanks to our proactive planning and the insights gained from that tabletop exercise.

By developing and regularly testing your incident response and business continuity plans, you can prepare your business to weather any storm, minimize the impact of disruptions, and ensure your continued success.

## CHAPTER 4: ZERO TRUST: NEVER TRUST, ALWAYS VERIFY

In the traditional model of cybersecurity, the focus was on building a strong perimeter around your network, like a castle with fortified walls. But in today's world of cloud computing, remote work, and mobile devices, that perimeter has become porous. Employees access company data from various locations and devices, blurring the lines between inside and outside the network.

This is where Zero Trust comes in. It's a security framework that assumes no user or device can be trusted by default, even those already inside the network. Instead, every access request is verified, regardless of where it originates.

Think of Zero Trust as a security philosophy that says, "Never trust, always verify." It's like having a vigilant guard at every door within your castle, constantly checking credentials and ensuring that only authorized individuals can access specific areas.

### THE CORE PRINCIPLES OF ZERO TRUST

Zero Trust is built on several key principles:

- Explicit Verification: Every user and device must be authenticated and authorized before accessing any resources, regardless of their location or network. This might involve using strong passwords, multi-factor authentication, or device certificates.
- Least Privilege Access: Users are granted only the minimum necessary access to perform their tasks. This limits the potential damage if an account is compromised.
- Microsegmentation: The network is divided into smaller, isolated segments, limiting the blast radius if one segment is compromised. This prevents attackers from moving laterally within the network.
- Continuous Monitoring: Systems and user behavior are continuously monitored for suspicious activity. This helps detect and respond to threats quickly.

## BENEFITS OF ZERO TRUST

Implementing a Zero Trust framework can provide significant security benefits:

- Reduced Attack Surface: By verifying every access request, Zero Trust reduces the opportunities for attackers to exploit vulnerabilities.
- Improved Data Protection: Zero Trust helps protect sensitive data by limiting access to only authorized users and devices.
- Enhanced Security Posture: Zero Trust creates a more proactive and resilient security posture, making it more difficult for attackers to succeed.
- Better Compliance: Zero Trust can help organizations comply with data privacy regulations and industry standards.

## IMPLEMENTING ZERO TRUST

Implementing a Zero Trust framework requires a shift in mindset and a combination of technology and processes. Here are some key steps:

- Assess Your Current Security Posture: Identify your assets, vulnerabilities, and current security controls.
- Define Your Zero Trust Strategy: Develop a plan for implementing Zero Trust, outlining your goals, priorities, and timelines.
- Implement Zero Trust Technologies: Deploy technologies like multi-factor authentication, identity and access management (IAM) solutions, and microsegmentation tools.
- Monitor and Adapt: Continuously monitor your systems and user behavior for suspicious activity. Adapt your Zero Trust framework as needed to address new threats and challenges.

## Validating Device/User Location and Ensuring Authorized Access

In a Zero Trust environment, it's crucial to verify not only the identity of users and devices but also their location and authorization status. This helps prevent unauthorized access from compromised devices or suspicious locations.

- Geo-IP Location Validation:
  - Zero Trust agents can validate the geographic IP location of the device or user attempting to access resources. This helps identify potentially risky login attempts from unusual or unexpected locations.
  - For example, if an employee typically works from Canada but suddenly tries to access company systems from Russia, the Zero Trust agent might flag this as suspicious and require additional verification.
- Authorized Device Verification:
  - Zero Trust solutions can ensure that only authorized devices can access company systems and data. This can be implemented through:

- Whitelisting: Only devices that are explicitly registered and approved can connect to the network.
- Endpoint Verification: Devices must meet certain security criteria, such as having up-to-date antivirus software and operating system patches, before being granted access.

- Tools and Technologies:
  - VPNs (Virtual Private Networks): VPNs can be used to create secure connections between devices and the company network, encrypting traffic and masking the user's actual IP address. This can be helpful for remote employees accessing sensitive data.
  - Zero Trust Agents: Zero Trust agents are software applications installed on devices that enforce access policies and validate user and device identity, location, and authorization status. Examples include Zscaler Private Access (ZPA), Cloudflare Zero Trust, and Cisco Duo Security.
  - Browser Extensions: Browser extensions like Google's BeyondCorp can enforce access policies and provide secure access to web applications, regardless of the user's location or device.

**Illustrative Scenario:**

A healthcare organization implements a Zero Trust framework to protect sensitive patient data. They deploy multi-factor authentication for all user accounts, implement role-based access control to limit data access, and segment their network to isolate critical systems. They also use security information and event management (SIEM) tools to monitor network activity for suspicious behavior.

This proactive approach helps them prevent data breaches, comply with HIPAA regulations, and maintain patient trust.

By adopting a Zero Trust mindset and implementing the appropriate technologies and processes, you can significantly strengthen your organization's security posture and protect your valuable assets in today's dynamic threat landscape.

## CHAPTER 5: BUILDING A CYBERSECURITY CULTURE: YOUR HUMAN FIREWALL

Imagine your employees as the individual cells within your company's immune system. Each cell plays a role in defending the body against harmful invaders. In the same way, every employee contributes to your company's cybersecurity defenses, forming a collective "human firewall" against cyber threats.

Building a strong cybersecurity culture is about more than just implementing technology and policies. It's about fostering a mindset of shared responsibility, where everyone understands their role in protecting the organization from cyberattacks.

Think of it like this: Even the strongest castle walls are vulnerable if the guards fall asleep on duty or leave the gates unlocked. Your employees are your frontline defenders, and their actions can significantly impact your overall security posture.

### LEADERSHIP SETS THE TONE

While IT plays a crucial role in implementing and managing cybersecurity measures, a truly effective cybersecurity culture starts at the top. When leaders prioritize and champion cybersecurity, it sends a powerful message to the entire organization.

Here's how leaders can set the tone for a security-conscious culture:

- Communicate the Importance of Cybersecurity: Clearly communicate the importance of cybersecurity to all employees, emphasizing its role in protecting the company, its customers, and its reputation.

- Lead by Example: Demonstrate good cybersecurity practices themselves, such as using strong passwords, being cautious with emails, and following security protocols.
- Invest in Cybersecurity: Allocate adequate resources for cybersecurity training, awareness programs, and technology.
- Integrate Security into Business Processes: Incorporate security considerations into all business decisions and processes, not just IT-related ones.
- Empower Employees: Empower employees to take ownership of cybersecurity by providing them with the knowledge, tools, and authority to make secure decisions.

## KEY ELEMENTS OF A CYBERSECURITY CULTURE

- Shared Responsibility: Cultivate a sense of shared responsibility for cybersecurity, where everyone understands that their actions can affect the organization's security. This means encouraging employees to report suspicious emails, use strong passwords, and follow security protocols.
- Open Communication: Create an environment where employees feel comfortable reporting security concerns or incidents without fear of blame. This helps identify and address vulnerabilities quickly.
- Continuous Training: Provide regular cybersecurity training and awareness programs to keep employees informed about the latest threats and best practices. This might include phishing simulations, security awareness videos, or interactive workshops.
- Recognition and Rewards: Recognize and reward employees who demonstrate good cybersecurity practices. This reinforces positive behavior and encourages a security-conscious mindset.

### Illustrative Scenarios

To better understand how these principles can be put into action, let's explore a few scenarios that demonstrate the diverse approaches organizations are taking to build a strong cybersecurity culture.

- Technology Startup:

  A fast-growing tech startup recognized the importance of embedding a security-first mindset from the very beginning. Instead of relying solely on traditional training methods, they integrated cybersecurity awareness into their daily routines.

  During their weekly all-hands meetings, they dedicated a brief segment to cybersecurity tips, highlighting real-world examples of cyberattacks and demonstrating how employees could protect themselves and the company. They also encouraged employees to share their own security-related experiences and ask questions, fostering open communication and collective learning.

  Recognizing that their employees were tech-savvy and appreciated a challenge, they introduced a "bug bounty" program. Employees were rewarded for identifying and reporting vulnerabilities in the company's systems and applications. This not only improved their security posture but also fostered a sense of ownership and engagement among employees.

  To stay ahead of emerging threats, they subscribed to threat intelligence feeds and shared relevant information with employees through a dedicated Slack channel. This kept employees informed about the latest phishing scams, malware campaigns, and vulnerabilities, empowering them to make informed decisions and protect themselves and the company.

- Retail Company:

  A retail chain with a large, dispersed workforce faced the

challenge of engaging employees in cybersecurity awareness. They decided to take a gamified approach, transforming their training program into an interactive competition.

They partnered with a cybersecurity training provider to create a custom online platform with modules on various security topics, such as phishing awareness, password security, and data protection. Employees earned points and badges for completing modules, passing quizzes, and participating in challenges.

To further boost engagement, they introduced a leaderboard, showcasing the top performers across different departments and locations. This friendly competition motivated employees to actively participate in the training and learn about cybersecurity in a fun and interactive way.

They also organized regular "cybersecurity awareness days" at their stores, featuring interactive games, quizzes, and giveaways. This helped bring cybersecurity to the forefront and reinforced the message that everyone plays a role in protecting the company and its customers.

As a result of these initiatives, the retail chain saw a significant improvement in employee awareness and a reduction in security incidents. Employees became more vigilant about phishing scams, used stronger passwords, and reported suspicious activity more readily.

**Deep Dive: Communication Strategies**

Effective communication is essential for building a cybersecurity culture. Here are some key strategies:

- Keep it Simple: Imagine trying to explain the offside rule in soccer to someone who's never seen a game. You wouldn't bombard them with technical terms and diagrams, would you? Instead, you'd use simple language and relatable examples to help them understand. The same principle applies to cybersecurity communication. Use clear, concise language that everyone can understand, avoiding technical jargon that might leave employees feeling lost and confused. Explain complex concepts in plain terms, using analogies or real-life examples to make them relatable.
- Make it Relevant: Connect cybersecurity concepts to employees' everyday work and personal lives, showing them how security impacts them directly.
- Use Multiple Channels: Don't rely on just one communication channel. Utilize a variety of methods to reach employees, such as emails, newsletters, posters, intranet articles, and team meetings.
- Encourage Two-Way Communication: Communication shouldn't be a one-way street. Create opportunities for employees to ask questions, share concerns, and provide feedback on security initiatives. This might involve regular Q&A sessions, feedback mechanisms, or an open-door policy.

## Deep Dive: Training Programs

Cybersecurity training should be engaging, informative, and tailored to different roles and responsibilities. Consider these approaches:

- Interactive Modules: Use online modules with quizzes, games, and simulations to make learning fun and interactive.
- Role-Based Training: Provide specific training for different roles, such as employees who handle sensitive data, those who work remotely, or those with administrative access.
- Regular Refresher Training: Offer refresher training periodically to reinforce key concepts and address new threats.

- In-Person Workshops or Webinars: While online modules offer flexibility and convenience, consider incorporating in-person workshops or webinars for more interactive and engaging learning experiences.

## Deep Dive: Reward Systems

Recognizing and rewarding good cybersecurity behavior can be a powerful motivator. Consider these ideas:

- Employee Recognition Programs: Publicly acknowledge and appreciate employees who demonstrate good security practices.
- Incentive Programs: Offer small incentives to encourage employees to participate in cybersecurity initiatives.
- Gamification: Incorporate gamification techniques into your cybersecurity training and awareness programs.

## Call to Action

Building a robust cybersecurity culture is an ongoing journey, not a destination. It requires continuous effort, communication, and adaptation. But the rewards are well worth the investment.

Remember, your employees are your first line of defense against cyber threats. By empowering them with knowledge, tools, and a sense of shared responsibility, you create a human firewall that complements your technology and policies.

Here are some key takeaways for building a cybersecurity culture in your organization:

- Start at the Top: Secure leadership buy-in and make cybersecurity a priority for the entire organization.
- Empower Your Employees: Provide employees with the knowledge, tools, and authority to make secure decisions.
- Communicate Effectively: Keep employees informed about security threats and best practices through various channels.

- Provide Ongoing Training: Offer engaging and relevant cybersecurity training programs tailored to different roles.
- Recognize and Reward: Acknowledge and reward employees who demonstrate good cybersecurity practices.

Take action today. Start by assessing your current cybersecurity culture. Identify areas for improvement and develop a plan to address them. Communicate your commitment to cybersecurity to all employees and provide them with the resources they need to be active participants in your security efforts.

By fostering a strong cybersecurity culture, you create a resilient and secure environment where your business can thrive.

# CHAPTER 6: CYBERSECURITY INSURANCE: YOUR FINANCIAL SAFETY NET

Imagine this: Despite your best efforts to build a strong cybersecurity fortress, a cunning attacker manages to breach your defenses. They deploy ransomware, encrypting your critical data and demanding a hefty ransom. Or perhaps they infiltrate your systems, stealing sensitive customer information and exposing you to potential lawsuits and regulatory fines.

While no security measure is foolproof, cybersecurity insurance can act as a financial safety net, helping you recover from the financial repercussions of a cyberattack. It's like having a backup generator for your business, ready to kick in when the power goes out.

## WHAT IS CYBERSECURITY INSURANCE?

Cybersecurity insurance is a specialized type of insurance that helps businesses mitigate the financial losses associated with cyberattacks. It covers a range of expenses, including:

- Data recovery: The cost of restoring data after a ransomware attack or data breach.

- Cyber extortion: Paying ransom demands to regain access to encrypted data.
- Legal fees: The cost of hiring lawyers to defend against lawsuits or regulatory actions.
- Notification costs: The expense of notifying affected customers about a data breach.
- Public relations: Hiring a PR firm to manage reputational damage.
- Business interruption: Lost income due to downtime caused by a cyberattack.

## What to Look for in a Cybersecurity Insurance Policy

Not all cybersecurity insurance policies are created equal. When choosing a policy, consider these factors:

- Coverage: Ensure the policy covers the specific types of cyberattacks your business is most vulnerable to, such as ransomware, phishing, and denial-of-service attacks.
- Limits: Understand the policy's coverage limits. These limits determine the maximum amount the insurer will pay for a covered claim.
- Deductibles: Determine the deductible amount, which is the amount you'll have to pay out-of-pocket before the insurance coverage kicks in.
- Exclusions: Pay close attention to the policy's exclusions. These are specific events or circumstances that are not covered by the policy.
- Premiums: Compare premiums from different insurers to find a policy that fits your budget.
- Claims Process: Understand the insurer's claims process and how they handle cybersecurity incidents.
- Breach Coach: Many policies include access to a breach coach, a cybersecurity expert who can guide you through the incident response process.
- Tip: Leverage Audits and Certifications:
  - Undergoing third-party audits or obtaining certifications can often lead to more favorable

insurance rates. These demonstrate a strong security posture and reduce the insurer's perceived risk.

o While these initiatives require effort and investment, consider tackling them early on, especially for startups, before processes become ingrained and more challenging to change.

o SOC 2 Type 2 Audit: This audit examines the effectiveness of your security controls over a period of time (usually 6-12 months). It assesses how well you protect customer data based on five trust service principles: security, availability, processing integrity, confidentiality, and privacy. A SOC 2 Type 2 report provides detailed information about your security controls and their effectiveness, giving insurers confidence in your ability to manage cyber risks.

o

o ISO 27001 Certification: This internationally recognized standard provides a framework for establishing, implementing, maintaining, and continually improving an information security management system (ISMS). It covers a broad range of security controls, including risk management, access control, data encryption, and incident response. Achieving ISO 27001 certification demonstrates your commitment to information security and can lead to lower insurance premiums.

o

## Benefits of Cybersecurity Insurance: More Than Just a Paycheck

Cybersecurity insurance provides more than just financial reimbursement in the event of a cyberattack. It offers a range of benefits that can help businesses recover, rebuild, and strengthen their resilience. Think of it as a comprehensive support system, ready to assist you when you need it most.

- **Financial Protection:**

- o This is the most obvious benefit. Cybersecurity insurance helps cover the costs associated with a cyberattack, which can quickly spiral into a financial crisis.
- o Without insurance, these costs could cripple a small business, forcing them to close their doors. Cybersecurity insurance provides a financial safety net, allowing you to recover and rebuild after an attack.
- **Peace of Mind:**
  - o Knowing you have a financial safety net in place can provide invaluable peace of mind. This allows you to focus on running your business, innovating, and serving your customers, without constantly worrying about the "what ifs" of a cyberattack.
- **Expert Support:**
  - o Many cybersecurity insurance policies include access to a network of experts who can assist you in the event of a cyberattack.
  - o Having access to this expertise can be invaluable, especially for small businesses that may not have dedicated cybersecurity staff.
- **Reputation Management:**
  - o A cyberattack can severely damage your company's reputation. Cybersecurity insurance can help mitigate this damage.
- **Competitive Advantage:**
  - o In today's digital world, cybersecurity is a key differentiator. Having cybersecurity insurance can signal to your stakeholders that you take security seriously.
- **Tip: Protect Your Policy:**
  - o Treat your cybersecurity insurance policy like any other sensitive document—keep it secure!
  - o Why? Because some ransomware attackers specifically seek out insurance policies to gauge a company's financial capacity.

## Limitations of Cybersecurity Insurance: Not a Silver Bullet

While cybersecurity insurance offers valuable protection, it's crucial to understand its limitations. It's not a magic shield that makes you invulnerable to cyberattacks, nor is it a replacement for proactive security measures.

- **Not a Substitute for Prevention:**
  - Cybersecurity insurance is designed to help you recover from the financial impact of a cyberattack, but it's not a replacement for proactive security measures.
- **Exclusions:**
  - Cybersecurity insurance policies often have exclusions – specific events or circumstances that are not covered by the policy.
- **Premiums:**
  - Cybersecurity insurance premiums can be expensive, especially for businesses with high-risk profiles.
- **Claim Denials:**
  - Even if you have cybersecurity insurance, there's no guarantee that your claim will be approved.

### Making a Claim: Navigating the Aftermath

Imagine the worst-case scenario: Despite your best efforts, your business has suffered a cyberattack. Now, you need to navigate the claims process to get the financial support you need to recover.

1. **Report the Incident Promptly:**
   a. Time is of the essence.
2. **Cooperate with the Insurer's Investigation:**
   a. The insurer will likely conduct an investigation.
   b. **Chain of Custody:** Be prepared to demonstrate a clear "chain of custody" for any evidence related to the cyberattack.
3. **Document Your Losses:**
   a. Keep detailed records.
4. **Mitigate Further Damage:**

      a. Take steps to mitigate further damage.
5. **Review the Insurer's Decision:**
      a. Once the insurer has completed their investigation, they will make a decision.

**Tips for a Smooth Claims Process:**

- **Understand Your Policy:** Familiarize yourself with your policy.
- **Keep Detailed Records:** Maintain thorough records.
- **Work with a Breach Coach:** Utilize their expertise.
- **Be Prepared:** Develop an incident response plan.

**Key Takeaways: Shielding Your Business with Cybersecurity Insurance**

Cybersecurity insurance is a critical component of a comprehensive cybersecurity strategy.

- **Understand the Basics:** It covers expenses associated with cyberattacks.
- **Choose Wisely:** Select a policy that aligns with your needs.
- **Proactive Security is Key:** Don't rely solely on insurance.
- **Be Prepared:** Develop an incident response plan.
- **Secure Your Policy:** Protect your insurance policy document.

# CHAPTER 7: CYBERSECURITY PITFALLS TO AVOID: DON'T FALL INTO THESE TRAPS

Even with the best intentions and a solid understanding of cybersecurity principles, it's easy to fall into common traps that can undermine your security efforts. Think of this chapter as your guide to navigating the cybersecurity minefield, helping you avoid those hidden dangers that can explode and cause significant damage to your business.

We'll explore a range of common pitfalls, from neglecting software updates to oversharing on social media, and provide practical tips on how to steer clear of these hazards.

## 1. Neglecting Software Updates: Don't Be a Sitting Duck

Imagine your software as a castle wall, protecting your valuable data and systems. Over time, cracks and weaknesses can appear in this wall, leaving you vulnerable to attacks. Software updates are like patching those cracks, reinforcing your defenses and keeping the invaders at bay.

Neglecting software updates is like leaving your castle walls crumbling, inviting attackers to exploit those weaknesses. Outdated software often contains known vulnerabilities that hackers can easily exploit to gain unauthorized access, steal data, or disrupt your operations.

**How to Avoid This Pitfall:**

- Enable Automatic Updates: Configure your operating systems and applications to automatically download and install updates. This ensures you always have the latest security patches.
- Schedule Regular Updates: If automatic updates aren't feasible, schedule regular maintenance windows to manually update your software.
- Prioritize Critical Updates: Pay close attention to critical security updates and install them as soon as possible.
- Use a Patch Management System: For larger organizations, consider using a patch management system to automate and streamline the patching process.

## 2. Falling for Phishing Scams: Don't Take the Bait

Phishing scams are like digital lures, designed to entice you with tempting offers or alarming threats, hoping you'll bite and reveal your sensitive information. These scams can arrive via email, text message, or even phone calls.

Falling for a phishing scam is like giving the keys to your castle to a cunning thief disguised as a friendly visitor. They can use your stolen information to access your accounts, steal your data, or even take over your entire system.

**How to Avoid This Pitfall:**

- Be Suspicious: Treat any unsolicited requests for personal information with skepticism, even if they appear to come from a trusted source. Look for red flags, such as:
    - Urgent or threatening language: Phishing emails often create a sense of urgency or fear to pressure you into acting quickly without thinking.
    - Generic greetings: Phishing emails may use generic greetings like "Dear Customer" or "Valued User" instead of your name.
    - Grammar and spelling errors: Phishing emails often contain grammatical errors, typos, or awkward phrasing.
    - Suspicious links or attachments: Hover over links to see the actual destination before clicking. Be wary of attachments, especially from unknown senders.
    - Requests for personal information: Legitimate organizations will rarely ask for sensitive information like passwords or credit card numbers via email.
- Verify the Sender: Double-check the sender's email address or phone number to ensure it's legitimate. Pay close attention to the domain name and look for any misspellings or variations.
- Don't Click on Suspicious Links: If you're unsure about a link, don't click on it. Instead, type the website address directly into your browser or use a search engine to find the official website.
- Beware of Attachments: Never open attachments from unknown senders. If you're expecting an attachment from

someone you know, confirm with them directly before opening it.

- Report Suspicious Activity: If you suspect a phishing attempt, report it to your IT department or security team. This helps them stay informed about current phishing campaigns and take steps to protect the organization.
- Enable Spam Filters: Use spam filters to block unwanted and potentially harmful emails. Most email providers offer built-in spam filters, but you can also implement additional filtering solutions for enhanced protection.
- Stay Informed: Keep up-to-date on the latest phishing techniques and trends. Share this information with your employees to help them recognize and avoid these scams.

By following these tips and staying vigilant, you can avoid falling prey to phishing scams and protect your business from their harmful consequences.

## 3. RELYING ON PASSWORDS ALONE: THE SINGLE KEY RISK

Imagine your passwords as the sole key to your castle. If someone gets hold of that key, they have complete access to everything inside. Relying on passwords alone is a risky strategy in today's cybersecurity landscape.

While strong passwords are essential (as discussed in Chapter 2), they are no longer enough to guarantee protection. Passwords can be stolen, guessed, or leaked in data breaches, leaving your accounts vulnerable to unauthorized access.

### Why MFA is a Must

Multi-factor authentication (MFA) adds an extra layer of security, like having a second lock on your castle door. Even if someone manages to steal or guess your key (password), they won't be able to get inside without the second key (the second authentication factor).

MFA requires users to provide multiple forms of authentication to verify their identity. This typically involves something you know (your password), something you have (a code generated by an app or sent to your phone), or something you are (biometric data like a fingerprint or facial scan).

**Benefits of MFA**

- Stronger Security: MFA significantly reduces the risk of unauthorized access, even if your password is compromised.
- Protection Against Password Leaks: If your password is leaked in a data breach, MFA prevents attackers from using it to access your accounts.
- Peace of Mind: Knowing you have an extra layer of security can provide peace of mind and reduce anxiety about cyberattacks.
- Increased Trust: Implementing MFA demonstrates to your customers and partners that you take security seriously and are committed to protecting their data.

**Implementing MFA**

Many online services and applications offer MFA options. Encourage your employees to enable MFA wherever possible, especially for critical accounts like email, banking, and social media.

You can also implement MFA for access to your company's internal systems and networks. This adds an extra layer of protection for your sensitive data and prevents unauthorized access.

Don't rely on passwords alone. Make MFA a mandatory part of your cybersecurity strategy.

## 4. Overlooking Mobile Device Security: The Pocket-Sized Risk

In today's mobile-first world, smartphones and tablets are essential business tools. But they're also vulnerable to cyberattacks, especially if they're not properly secured.

Think of your mobile devices as mini-offices that you carry around in your pocket. They contain sensitive data, access your company network, and store valuable information. Failing to secure these devices is like leaving your office unlocked and unattended, inviting thieves to walk in and take what they want.

## Why Mobile Device Security Matters

Mobile devices face unique security challenges:

- Loss or Theft: Smartphones and tablets are easily lost or stolen, potentially exposing your data to unauthorized access.
- Public Wi-Fi Risks: Connecting to unsecured public Wi-Fi networks can leave your devices vulnerable to eavesdropping and attacks.
- Malicious Apps: Downloading malicious apps from untrusted sources can infect your devices with malware and compromise your data.
- Outdated Operating Systems: Failing to update your mobile operating system can leave your devices vulnerable to known exploits.

## How to Avoid This Pitfall

- Strong Passwords and Biometrics: Require strong passwords or biometric authentication (fingerprint, facial recognition) to unlock devices and access sensitive apps.
- Encryption: Enable device encryption to protect data in case of loss or theft.
- Mobile Device Management (MDM): Consider implementing an MDM solution to manage and secure company-owned devices. MDM solutions allow you to:
  - Enforce security policies, such as password requirements and app restrictions.

- o   Remotely lock or wipe lost or stolen devices.
- o   Install and update software remotely.
- o   Monitor device activity for suspicious behavior.
- Secure Wi-Fi Usage: Educate employees about the risks of using public Wi-Fi and encourage them to use a VPN (Virtual Private Network) to encrypt their connections.
- App Security: Only download apps from trusted sources, such as the official app stores. Be cautious of apps that request excessive permissions or access to sensitive data.
- Regular Updates: Keep your mobile operating system and apps up to date to patch security vulnerabilities.

## BYOD: Balancing Convenience and Security

Many organizations allow employees to use their personal devices for work, a practice known as Bring Your Own Device (BYOD). While BYOD offers convenience and flexibility, it also introduces security challenges.

If your organization allows or is considering BYOD, it's crucial to implement an effective BYOD policy and security measures to protect company data and systems.

## Key Considerations for BYOD

- Acceptable Use Policy: Clearly define what constitutes acceptable use of personal devices for work purposes. This might include restrictions on accessing certain websites, downloading apps, or storing sensitive data.
- Device Enrollment: Establish a process for enrolling personal devices in your company's mobile device management (MDM) system. This allows you to enforce security policies and monitor device activity.
- Data Separation: Implement solutions that separate personal and work data on devices. This might involve using containerization technologies or separate work profiles.
- Security Software: Require employees to install security software, such as antivirus and anti-malware, on their personal devices.

- Password Protection: Enforce strong password requirements or biometric authentication for all devices.
- Network Access Control: Implement network access control measures to restrict access to your company network based on device compliance with security policies.
- Data Encryption: Require encryption for all sensitive data stored on personal devices.
- Remote Wipe: Ensure you have the ability to remotely wipe company data from personal devices if they are lost, stolen, or the employee leaves the company.
- Employee Education: Train employees on BYOD security best practices, such as avoiding unsecured Wi-Fi networks, only downloading apps from trusted sources, and reporting lost or stolen devices immediately.

**Mobile Device Management (MDM) Solutions for BYOD**

Several MDM solutions are available to help you manage and secure personal devices used for work. Some popular options include:

- Google Workspace MDM: This cloud-based solution allows you to manage Android and iOS devices, enforcing security policies, deploying apps, and securing data.
- Microsoft Intune: A comprehensive MDM solution that supports various devices, including iOS, Android, Windows, and macOS. It offers features like device enrollment, app management, and data protection.
- VMware Workspace ONE: A unified endpoint management platform that provides comprehensive device management, application management, and security capabilities.

These MDM solutions can help you secure personal devices used for work, ensuring that company data is protected and compliance requirements are met.

## 5. Misconfiguring Cloud Services: Leaving the Drawbridge Down

Imagine your cloud services as a majestic castle in the digital realm. You've built strong walls and fortified gates, but you accidentally leave the drawbridge down, allowing anyone to stroll right into your inner sanctum.

Misconfiguring cloud services is like leaving that drawbridge down, creating a gaping security hole that attackers can exploit. Cloud services offer immense power and flexibility, but they also introduce unique security challenges. If not configured correctly, they can become entry points for cyberattacks, leading to data breaches, service disruptions, and financial losses.

## Common Cloud Misconfigurations

- Unrestricted Access: Failing to properly configure access controls can allow unauthorized users to access sensitive data or take control of critical systems.
- Lack of Encryption: Leaving data unencrypted in the cloud makes it vulnerable to theft or exposure in case of a breach.
- Open Ports and Services: Leaving unnecessary ports and services open on your cloud servers can provide attackers with entry points.
- Default Credentials: Failing to change default passwords or usernames can make it easy for attackers to gain access.
- Lack of Monitoring: Not monitoring your cloud environment for suspicious activity can allow attacks to go undetected.

## How to Avoid This Pitfall

- Follow Security Best Practices: Adhere to security best practices when configuring your cloud services. This includes:
    - Implementing strong access controls, including multi-factor authentication and role-based access control.
    - Encrypting data at rest and in transit.
    - Closing unnecessary ports and disabling unused services.
    - Changing default credentials and using strong, unique passwords.

- o Enabling logging and monitoring to detect suspicious activity.
- Regularly Review Configurations: Periodically review your cloud configurations to ensure they align with your security policies and industry best practices.
- Use Configuration Management Tools: Consider using configuration management tools to automate and streamline the process of configuring and securing your cloud services.
- Stay Informed: Keep up-to-date on the latest cloud security threats and vulnerabilities. Cloud providers often release security advisories and updates to address emerging threats.

By taking these steps to secure your cloud configurations, you can raise the drawbridge, protect your digital castle, and keep your business safe in the cloud.

## 6. IGNORING PHYSICAL SECURITY: THE REAL-WORLD WEAK POINT

In our increasingly digital world, it's easy to focus solely on cybersecurity and overlook the importance of physical security. But remember, physical security is still a critical component of your overall protection strategy.

Think of your physical assets – your office, your data center, your equipment – as the foundation of your digital fortress. If someone can gain physical access to these assets, they can bypass your digital defenses and cause significant damage.

**Why Physical Security Matters**

- Data Theft: A thief could steal computers, servers, or storage devices containing sensitive data.
- Device Tampering: An intruder could tamper with your equipment, installing malware or compromising your network.
- Sabotage: A disgruntled employee or malicious actor could damage or destroy your critical infrastructure.

- Social Engineering: An attacker could gain physical access to your premises through social engineering tactics, posing as a delivery person or a maintenance worker.

## How to Avoid This Pitfall

- Secure Your Premises:
    - Implement access controls, such as keycard systems, security guards, and visitor logs, to restrict access to your office and data center.
    - Install surveillance cameras to monitor activity and deter intruders.
    - Use alarms and intrusion detection systems to alert you of unauthorized access.
- Protect Your Equipment:
    - Securely store laptops, mobile devices, and other portable equipment when not in use.
    - Use cable locks or other physical security measures to prevent theft.
    - Consider using biometric authentication or other access controls for sensitive devices.
- Employee Awareness:
    - Train employees on physical security best practices, such as:
        - Keeping their workstations secure when unattended.
        - Reporting suspicious activity or unauthorized individuals.
        - Following proper procedures for handling sensitive documents and equipment.
- Data Center Security:
    - If you have a data center, implement strict access controls, environmental monitoring, and fire suppression systems.
    - Consider using a colocation facility or cloud provider with robust physical security measures.
    - Man Traps: For high-security areas like data centers, consider implementing man traps. These are small,

enclosed spaces with two sets of interlocking doors. The first door must close before the second door can open, preventing tailgating and ensuring that only authorized individuals can enter. Man traps can be combined with access control systems, such as keycard readers or biometric scanners, to further enhance security.

- Defensive Office Design: The way your office is designed can play a role in your physical security. Consider incorporating these defensive design elements:
    o Natural Surveillance: Position workstations and common areas to allow for natural surveillance and visibility. This can deter unauthorized access and make it easier to spot suspicious activity.
    o Access Control Points: Strategically place access control points, such as reception desks or security checkpoints, to control entry and monitor visitor flow.
    o Perimeter Security: Secure the perimeter of your office with fences, walls, or other barriers. Use landscaping to create natural barriers and deter intrusion.
    o Lighting: Ensure adequate lighting both inside and outside your office to deter crime and improve visibility.
    o Employee Training: Educate employees about defensive office design and encourage them to be mindful of security considerations in their workspace.

By incorporating these physical security measures, you can create a multi-layered defense that protects your business from both physical and digital threats.

## 7. FAILING TO BACK UP DATA: PLAYING WITH FIRE

Imagine your data as a precious collection of photographs, documents, and memories. Now imagine losing all those irreplaceable items in a fire or a flood. Failing to back up your data is like storing all your valuables in a single, vulnerable location, risking complete loss in case of disaster.

Data is the lifeblood of your business. It includes customer information, financial records, intellectual property, and operational data that keeps your business running smoothly. Losing this data can be devastating, leading to financial losses, business disruption, and reputational damage.

**Why Data Backups are Essential**

Data loss can occur due to various reasons:

- Hardware Failure: Hard drives can crash, servers can fail, and devices can malfunction, leading to data loss.
- Accidental Deletion: Employees can accidentally delete files or folders, or even entire databases.
- Ransomware Attacks: Ransomware can encrypt your data, making it inaccessible until you pay a ransom.
- Natural Disasters: Fires, floods, or other natural disasters can damage your equipment and destroy your data.
- Cyberattacks: Other types of cyberattacks, such as data breaches or malware infections, can also lead to data loss.

**How to Avoid This Pitfall**

6. Regular Backups: Back up your data regularly, depending on how often it changes and how critical it is to your business operations. Daily backups are recommended for essential data.
7. Multiple Backups: Create multiple backups and store them in different locations, such as:
   a. On-site backups: Store backups on a separate server or device in your office.

Off-site backups: Store backups in a secure off-site location, such as a safe deposit box or a separate data center. * Cloud backups: Use cloud storage services to back up your data to a secure, remote location.

- 3-2-1 Backup Rule: Follow the 3-2-1 backup rule:
    - Keep at least three copies of your data (original plus two backups).
    - Store your backups on two different media types (e.g., hard drive, tape, cloud).
    - Store at least one backup copy off-site or in the cloud.
- Test Your Backups: Regularly test your backups to ensure they are working correctly and that you can restore your data in case of an incident.
- Automate Backups: Use automated backup solutions to ensure consistency and avoid human error.
- Secure Your Backups: Protect your backups with strong passwords, encryption, and access controls.

## The Cloud vs. On-Premises: Where to Keep Your Backups

We've discussed the importance of data backups in other chapters (see Chapter 2). Now, let's explore the advantages of different backup locations:

- Cloud Backups:
    - Accessibility: Access your backups from anywhere with an internet connection.
    - Scalability: Easily scale your storage capacity as your needs change.
    - Disaster Recovery: Protect your data from physical disasters like fires or floods.
    - Cost-Effectiveness: Often more cost-effective than maintaining on-premises infrastructure.
- On-Premises Backups:
    - Control: Maintain complete control over your backup infrastructure.
    - Performance: Potentially faster backup and recovery speeds, depending on your network infrastructure.
    - Compliance: May be required for certain compliance regulations or industry standards.

Consider your specific needs, budget, and risk tolerance when choosing between cloud and on-premises backups. A hybrid approach, combining both cloud and on-premises storage, can provide the best of both worlds.

## 8. NEGLECTING EMPLOYEE TRAINING: LEAVING YOUR FRONT LINE UNPREPARED

Imagine your employees as the frontline soldiers defending your business from cyberattacks. Would you send them into battle without proper training and equipment? Neglecting employee training is like leaving your troops vulnerable and unprepared, increasing the risk of your defenses being breached.

Your employees are often the primary targets of cyberattacks. Phishing scams, social engineering tactics, and other malicious attempts often rely on human error to succeed. Without proper training and awareness, your employees can become unwitting accomplices to cybercriminals, inadvertently opening the doors to your valuable data and systems.

### Why Employee Training is Crucial

- Human Error: Human error is a leading cause of security breaches. Employees may fall victim to phishing scams, use weak passwords, or misconfigure systems, creating vulnerabilities that attackers can exploit.
- Social Engineering: Social engineering tactics prey on human psychology, manipulating employees into revealing sensitive information or granting unauthorized access.
- Insider Threats: While most employees are trustworthy, disgruntled or careless employees can pose a significant security risk.
- Evolving Threats: Cyber threats are constantly evolving. Regular training helps employees stay informed about the latest threats and how to protect themselves and the company.

## How to Avoid This Pitfall

- Regular Security Awareness Training: Provide regular, ongoing security awareness training to all employees. This training should cover topics such as:
  - Recognizing and avoiding phishing scams
  - Creating strong passwords and practicing good password hygiene
  - Protecting sensitive data and following data security policies
  - Identifying and reporting suspicious activity
  - Understanding the company's security policies and procedures
- Tailored Training: Offer specialized training for employees with specific roles or responsibilities, such as those who handle sensitive data or have administrative access.
- Engaging Training Methods: Use engaging and interactive training methods, such as simulations, games, and real-world examples, to make learning fun and effective.
- Reinforce Training: Regularly reinforce security awareness messages through emails, newsletters, posters, and other communication channels.
- Promote a Security Culture: Foster a culture of security awareness and responsibility, where employees feel empowered to report concerns and contribute to the organization's security posture.

By investing in comprehensive employee training and promoting a security-conscious culture, you can transform your employees from potential vulnerabilities into your strongest line of defense against cyber threats.

## 9. RELYING SOLELY ON TECHNOLOGY: THE HUMAN FACTOR FALLACY

In the realm of cybersecurity, it's easy to get caught up in the latest technologies, the shiny new tools, and the promise of impenetrable defenses. But cybersecurity is not just about technology; it's about people.

Relying solely on technology is like building a fortress with state-of-the-art defenses but forgetting to train the guards or establish clear protocols. Even the most sophisticated technology can be rendered useless if the human element is neglected.

**Why the Human Factor is Crucial**

- Social Engineering: Many cyberattacks rely on social engineering tactics, manipulating people into revealing sensitive information or granting unauthorized access. Technology alone cannot prevent these attacks; it requires human awareness and vigilance. Even the most sophisticated and expensive security controls can be bypassed by a clever social engineer who knows how to exploit human psychology and trust.
- Insider Threats: Even with the best technology in place, insider threats – whether malicious or unintentional – can pose a significant risk. Addressing insider threats requires a combination of technology, processes, and a strong security culture.
- Adaptability: The cybersecurity landscape is constantly evolving. Technology alone cannot keep up with the ever-changing threat landscape. It requires human intelligence, adaptability, and decision-making to respond to new challenges and refine security strategies.
- Security Awareness: Technology can provide tools and defenses, but it's ultimately up to humans to use them effectively. A security-conscious culture, where employees understand their role in protecting the organization, is essential for a robust cybersecurity posture.

**How to Avoid This Pitfall**

- Invest in Employee Training: Provide regular and engaging security awareness training to all employees, covering topics like phishing scams, social engineering, password security, and data protection.

- Build a Security Culture: Foster a culture of shared responsibility for cybersecurity, where employees feel empowered to report concerns, follow security protocols, and contribute to the organization's security posture.
- Balance Technology with Human Oversight: While technology plays a crucial role in cybersecurity, don't neglect the human element. Combine technological solutions with human oversight, such as security analysts who can monitor systems, analyze threats, and respond to incidents.
- Focus on Processes and Policies: Develop clear security policies and procedures that guide employee behavior and ensure consistent security practices.
- Communication and Collaboration: Encourage open communication and collaboration between IT and other departments to ensure that security considerations are integrated into all business processes.

By recognizing the human factor in cybersecurity and balancing technology with human awareness, training, and processes, you can create a truly resilient security posture that protects your business from the ever-evolving threat landscape.

## 10. Falling Behind on Security Awareness Training: The "Set It and Forget It" Trap

Imagine training your employees on cybersecurity once, then never revisiting it. It's like teaching your troops how to use a musket in the 18th century and then sending them into a modern battlefield with no further instruction.

Cybersecurity threats are constantly evolving. New attack methods emerge, social engineering tactics become more sophisticated, and vulnerabilities are discovered in even the most trusted software. Failing to keep your employees' security awareness up to date is like sending them into battle with outdated weapons and tactics.

## Why Ongoing Training is Essential

- New Threats: New malware, phishing scams, and social engineering techniques emerge constantly. Employees need to be aware of these evolving threats to protect themselves and the company.
- Reinforcement: Even with initial training, people forget. Regular refreshers reinforce key concepts and keep security top-of-mind.
- Changing Technology: As your company adopts new technologies and cloud services, employees need training on how to use them securely.
- Human Error: Human error is a leading cause of security breaches. Ongoing training helps minimize these errors by reinforcing best practices and promoting a security-conscious culture.

## How to Avoid This Pitfall

- Regular Training: Provide regular security awareness training to all employees, at least annually, and more frequently for those in high-risk roles.
- Variety of Methods: Use a variety of training methods to keep employees engaged, such as:
  - Online modules with quizzes and interactive scenarios
  - In-person workshops or webinars
  - Phishing simulations
  - Security awareness videos and newsletters
- Tailored Training: Provide role-based training to address the specific needs of different departments and job functions.
- Current and Relevant Content: Ensure your training materials are up-to-date and cover the latest threats and vulnerabilities.
- Reinforce Key Messages: Regularly reinforce security awareness messages through emails, posters, and other communication channels.

By investing in ongoing security awareness training, you empower your employees to be your first line of defense against cyber threats, ensuring they have the knowledge and skills to stay vigilant and protect your business.

## 11. Overspending on Security: The "More is Always Better" Myth

In the cybersecurity world, it's easy to fall into the trap of thinking that more spending equals more security. You might be tempted to buy every new gadget, subscribe to every threat intelligence feed, and implement every security control imaginable. But without a clear understanding of your risks and priorities, you could end up overspending on solutions that don't effectively address your specific needs.

Think of cybersecurity spending like investing in an army. You wouldn't just buy the most expensive weapons and armor without considering your specific needs, your enemy's tactics, and the terrain you're fighting on. Similarly, you shouldn't just throw money at cybersecurity solutions without a strategic approach.

### The Importance of Risk Assessment

A threat and risk assessment process helps you identify your critical assets, assess potential threats and vulnerabilities, and determine the likelihood and impact of various cyberattacks. This allows you to prioritize your security efforts and invest in solutions that provide the most effective protection for your specific needs.

### Understanding Residual Risk

No security measure is foolproof. Even with the best defenses in place, there will always be some level of residual risk – the risk that remains after you've implemented security controls.

The key is to understand the nature of that residual risk and its potential impact on your business. If the cost of mitigating a particular risk is higher than the potential impact of that risk, it might not be worth the investment.

**Avoiding the Cost Trap**

Here are some tips to avoid overspending on cybersecurity:

- Conduct a Risk Assessment: Identify your critical assets, threats, and vulnerabilities.
- Prioritize Your Efforts: Focus on mitigating the risks that pose the greatest threat to your business.
- Choose Cost-Effective Solutions: Don't assume that the most expensive solutions are always the best. Look for solutions that provide the necessary level of protection at a reasonable cost.
- Consider Open-Source Options: Many effective security tools are available as open-source software, which can significantly reduce costs.
- Leverage Cloud Services: Cloud-based security solutions can often be more cost-effective than on-premises solutions, especially for small businesses.
- Regularly Review Your Spending: Periodically review your cybersecurity spending to ensure it aligns with your current needs and priorities.

By taking a strategic approach to cybersecurity spending and understanding your risk profile, you can invest wisely in solutions that provide the most effective protection for your business without breaking the bank.

# CHAPTER 8: KEEPING YOUR BUSINESS SECURE: ONGOING STEPS

Imagine a military outpost in a hostile territory. You can't just build the fortifications and relax, assuming you're safe forever. You need to maintain constant vigilance, scout for enemy activity, reinforce your defenses, and adapt your strategies to counter new threats.

Cybersecurity is similar. It's not a one-time battle but an ongoing campaign that requires constant attention and adaptation.

In this chapter, we'll explore the essential steps to keep your business secure in the ever-changing digital landscape. Think of it as your field manual for maintaining a strong cybersecurity posture, where your business can operate effectively, protected from the constant barrage of cyberattacks.

## STAYING INFORMED: GATHERING INTELLIGENCE

In the military, intelligence gathering is crucial for understanding the enemy's capabilities, intentions, and tactics. The same applies to cybersecurity. You need to stay informed about the latest threats, vulnerabilities, and attack trends to effectively defend your business.

Think of yourself as a cybersecurity intelligence officer, constantly gathering information from various sources to stay ahead of the enemy.

Here are some ways to gather cybersecurity intelligence:

- Threat Intelligence Feeds: Subscribe to threat intelligence feeds from reputable sources, such as the Cybersecurity & Infrastructure Security Agency (CISA), the National Cyber Security Centre (NCSC), and industry-specific organizations. These feeds provide timely updates on emerging threats, vulnerabilities, and attack trends, like receiving real-time reports from reconnaissance missions.
  - Expand: Provide specific examples of threat intelligence platforms, such as Recorded Future, ThreatConnect, and Anomali. Briefly describe the types of information these platforms provide, such as malware analysis, vulnerability alerts, and threat actor profiles.
- Security Blogs and Newsletters: Follow cybersecurity blogs and newsletters from trusted experts and organizations. These resources offer insights into the latest security news,

best practices, and emerging technologies, similar to debriefing reports from the front lines.

- o Expand: Recommend specific blogs and newsletters, such as Krebs on Security, Schneier on Security, and Threatpost. Highlight the expertise and perspectives offered by these sources.
- Industry Events and Conferences: Attend cybersecurity events and conferences to learn from experts, network with peers, and stay abreast of the latest trends, much like attending military strategy meetings.
  - o Expand: Mention major cybersecurity conferences like RSA Conference, Black Hat, and DEF CON. Briefly describe the benefits of attending these events, such as gaining insights from keynote speakers, attending workshops and training sessions, and networking with industry professionals.
- Government Alerts and Advisories: Pay attention to alerts and advisories issued by government agencies, such as CISA and the FBI. These alerts often provide warnings about specific threats or vulnerabilities that could impact your business, acting as your early warning system.
  - o Expand: Provide specific examples of government alerts and advisories, such as CISA's Known Exploited Vulnerabilities Catalog and the FBI's Internet Crime Complaint Center (IC3) reports. Explain how these resources can help businesses prioritize patching and mitigation efforts.
- Open-Source Intelligence (OSINT): Leverage publicly available information, such as social media, news articles, and online forums, to gather intelligence about potential threats and vulnerabilities.
  - o Expand: Provide examples of OSINT tools and techniques, such as using social media monitoring tools to track mentions of your company or industry, and searching online forums for discussions about potential vulnerabilities in software you use.

## SECURITY ASSESSMENTS: CONDUCTING RECONNAISSANCE

Just as military forces conduct reconnaissance missions to assess the enemy's defenses and identify weaknesses, your business needs periodic security assessments to evaluate its cybersecurity posture. These assessments help you pinpoint vulnerabilities, assess your risk level, and prioritize security improvements.

Think of security assessments as your cybersecurity reconnaissance missions, providing valuable intel about your defenses and highlighting areas that need reinforcement.

Here are some types of security assessments to consider:

- Vulnerability Scans: These automated scans identify known vulnerabilities in your systems and applications, such as outdated software, misconfigurations, and security flaws, much like aerial surveillance to spot weaknesses in enemy fortifications.
  - Expand: Provide examples of vulnerability scanning tools, such as Nexpose, Nessus, QualysGuard, and OpenVAS. Briefly explain the different types of vulnerability scans, such as network scans, web application scans, and database scans.
- Penetration Testing: Ethical hackers simulate real-world attacks to identify weaknesses in your defenses and exploit vulnerabilities, acting as friendly forces probing your defenses to identify weak points.
  - Expand: Discuss the different types of penetration testing, such as black box testing, white box testing, and grey box testing. Explain the benefits of hiring external penetration testers to provide an objective assessment of your security posture.
- Risk Assessments: These assessments evaluate your overall risk profile, considering your assets, threats, vulnerabilities, and the potential impact of a cyberattack, similar to a strategic assessment of the battlefield.
  - Expand: Provide a more detailed explanation of the risk assessment process, including identifying assets, threats, and vulnerabilities, and calculating risk

scores. Mention different risk assessment methodologies, such as quantitative risk assessment and qualitative risk assessment.

- Security Audits: Independent audits assess your compliance with security standards and regulations, such as ISO 27001 or PCI DSS, ensuring your forces adhere to the rules of engagement.
  - o Expand: Provide examples of specific security standards and regulations, such as PCI DSS for payment card data, HIPAA for healthcare data, and GDPR for personal data of EU residents. Explain the benefits of conducting regular security audits to ensure compliance and demonstrate due diligence.

## ADAPTING TO THE EVOLVING LANDSCAPE: AGILE MANEUVERS

The digital battlefield is constantly changing, with new technologies emerging, business models evolving, and cyber threats becoming more sophisticated. To stay secure, your cybersecurity strategy must adapt to these changes with agility and precision.

Think of it like maneuvering your forces in response to enemy movements. You need to adjust your tactics, anticipate new attack vectors, and be prepared to deploy countermeasures.

Here are some ways to adapt your cybersecurity strategy:

- Embrace New Technologies: Stay informed about new security technologies and evaluate how they can enhance your defenses. This might include cloud-based security solutions, artificial intelligence (AI)-powered threat detection, or advanced endpoint protection, similar to upgrading your arsenal with new weapons and defenses.
  - o Expand: Provide specific examples of emerging security technologies, such as cloud-based security information and event management (SIEM) solutions, endpoint detection and response (EDR) tools, and threat intelligence platforms. Discuss how these

technologies can help businesses adapt to the changing threat landscape.

- Review Your Policies and Procedures: Regularly review and update your cybersecurity policies and procedures to reflect changes in your business environment, technology landscape, and regulatory requirements, much like updating your battle plans based on new intel.
  - o Expand: Provide examples of specific policies and procedures that should be regularly reviewed and updated, such as acceptable use policies, data breach response plans, and incident reporting procedures.
- Invest in Continuous Learning: Encourage your employees to continuously learn about cybersecurity, providing them with opportunities for training, education, and professional development, ensuring your troops are well-trained and prepared for new challenges.
  - o Expand: Suggest specific resources for employee cybersecurity training and education, such as online courses, certifications, and workshops. Encourage businesses to create a culture of continuous learning by providing employees with opportunities to stay informed about the latest security threats and best practices.
- Build a Culture of Adaptation: Foster a culture where employees are comfortable with change and embrace new security measures as they are implemented, creating a flexible and responsive force ready to adapt to any situation.
  * Expand: Provide examples of how businesses can foster a culture of adaptation, such as encouraging employees to share security-related news and information, rewarding employees for identifying vulnerabilities, and celebrating successes in preventing cyberattacks.

# CHAPTER 9: THE RISE OF THE MACHINES: AI AND THE FUTURE OF CYBERSECURITY

Artificial intelligence (AI) is rapidly transforming the world around us, including the cybersecurity landscape. AI is changing how we detect threats, protect our data, and respond to attacks.

## LARGE LANGUAGE MODELS (LLMs): A DOUBLE-EDGED SWORD

Large Language Models (LLMs), like ChatGPT, are a fascinating type of artificial intelligence. They come pre-trained on a massive dataset of text and code, which allows them to communicate and generate human-like responses to a wide range of prompts and questions. This makes them incredibly useful for tasks like summarizing factual topics, creating stories, and even generating different kinds of creative text formats.

What sets LLMs apart from traditional search engines is their ability to present information in a way that's almost ready for immediate use. Instead of simply providing a list of links or documents, LLMs can synthesize information, draw conclusions, and present it in a clear, concise, and human-like manner.

However, this ability also makes them potentially dangerous. Because LLMs can generate such convincing and human-like responses, it's easy to assume they are always correct or truthful. But LLMs can sometimes "hallucinate" or generate incorrect information, and they can even be manipulated to spread misinformation or propaganda. This highlights the importance of critical thinking and careful evaluation when interacting with LLMs.

By understanding the unique capabilities and potential risks of LLMs, businesses can harness their power while mitigating their potential downsides.

## UNDERSTANDING THE RISKS OF LLMs

- **Phishing and Social Engineering:** LLMs can be used by malicious actors to create highly convincing phishing emails, social media messages, or even generate fake websites that trick employees into revealing sensitive information or downloading malware.

- **Data Leakage:** If employees inadvertently share confidential information or proprietary code with an LLM, that data could be inadvertently incorporated into the model's training data and potentially exposed to others.
- **Misinformation and Manipulation:** LLMs can be used to generate and spread misinformation or propaganda, potentially damaging your company's reputation or influencing employee behavior.
- **Bias and Discrimination:** LLMs are trained on vast amounts of data, which may contain biases or reflect societal prejudices. If not carefully monitored, LLMs could perpetuate or even amplify these biases, leading to discriminatory outcomes.

## MITIGATING THE RISKS OF LLMS

- **Employee Education:** Train your employees on the potential risks of LLMs and how to use them safely and responsibly. Emphasize the importance of not sharing sensitive information with LLMs and being critical of the information they generate.
- **Access Controls:** Implement access controls to limit who can use LLMs and for what purposes. Consider restricting access to sensitive data or code that could be compromised if shared with an LLM.
- **Data Governance:** Establish clear data governance policies that address the use of LLMs and the protection of sensitive information. Ensure that employees understand the importance of data privacy and confidentiality when interacting with LLMs.
- **Provide an Approved LLM:** One of the most effective ways to mitigate the risks of LLMs is to provide your employees with an officially sanctioned and vetted LLM solution. This allows you to:
  - Control Data Access: Choose an LLM provider that prioritizes data security and privacy. Review their

data handling practices, encryption protocols, and access controls to ensure your sensitive information is protected.
- o Monitor Usage: Implement monitoring and auditing tools to track how employees are using the LLM and identify any potential risks or misuse.
- o Enforce Policies: Integrate the LLM with your company's security policies and data governance frameworks.
- o Reduce Shadow IT: By providing a secure and approved LLM, you reduce the likelihood of employees resorting to unapproved, potentially risky, free LLMs. Examples of enterprise-grade LLMs with robust security features include Google Gemini for business or enterprise and ChatGPT Enterprise. While these solutions require additional investment, the cost should be weighed against the potential risks of data leakage and security breaches associated with using free, unvetted LLMs.

## THE HUMAN FIREWALL FACTOR

The key to successfully navigating the LLM landscape is to combine the power of AI with the vigilance and critical thinking of your human firewall. By educating your employees about the risks and benefits of LLMs, empowering them to use these tools responsibly, and implementing appropriate security controls, you can harness the transformative potential of AI while mitigating its risks.

# APPENDIX: YOUR CYBERSECURITY TOOLKIT

This appendix provides a collection of resources, links to templates, and helpful information to further enhance your understanding of cybersecurity and assist you in implementing the practices outlined in this book.

**Cybersecurity Resources**

- **Government Agencies:**
    - Cybersecurity & Infrastructure Security Agency (CISA): cisa.gov - Provides alerts, advisories, and resources on cybersecurity threats and vulnerabilities.
    - Federal Bureau of Investigation (FBI): fbi.gov - Offers information on cybercrime, including reporting mechanisms and prevention tips.
    - National Cyber Security Centre (NCSC): ncsc.gov.uk - (If your target audience includes UK businesses) Provides guidance and support on cybersecurity for individuals and organizations.
    - Canadian Centre for Cyber Security: cyber.gc.ca - (Given your location) Offers resources, advice, and services to help Canadians be secure online.
- **Industry Organizations:**
    - National Institute of Standards and Technology (NIST): nist.gov - Develops cybersecurity standards, guidelines, and best practices.
    - SANS Institute: sans.org - Provides cybersecurity training, certifications, and research.
    - (ISC)²: isc2.org - Offers cybersecurity certifications and resources for professionals.
    - Cloud Security Alliance (CSA): cloudsecurityalliance.org - Provides guidance and best practices for cloud security.
- **Other Resources:**
    - Cybersecurity Information Sharing Act (CISA) Resources: www.cisa.gov/cisa-resources [invalid URL removed]
    - National Cybersecurity Awareness Month: www.cisa.gov/national-cybersecurity-awareness-month [invalid URL removed]
    - Stay Safe Online: staysafeonline.org

**Glossary of Key Terms**

- **Antivirus Software:** Software that detects and removes malware from your computer.
- **Cybersecurity:** The practice of protecting computer systems and networks from unauthorized access, use, disclosure, disruption, modification, or destruction.
- **Data Breach:** An incident in which sensitive, protected, or confidential data is copied, transmitted, viewed, stolen, or used by an unauthorized individual.
- **Encryption:** The process of converting data into a coded format to prevent unauthorized access.
- **Firewall:** A network security device that monitors and controls incoming and outgoing network traffic.
- **Malware:** Malicious software, such as viruses, worms, and ransomware, designed to harm or disrupt computer systems.
- **Multi-Factor Authentication (MFA):** A security measure that requires users to provide multiple forms of authentication to verify their identity.
- **Phishing:** A type of social engineering attack that uses deceptive emails or websites to trick individuals into revealing sensitive information.
- **Ransomware:** A type of malware that encrypts data and demands a ransom payment to restore access.
- **Zero Trust:** A security framework that assumes no user or device can be trusted by default, even those already inside the network.

**Templates**

- **Cybersecurity Policy Templates:** SANS.org, a leading provider of cybersecurity training and resources, offers a collection of free cybersecurity policy templates on their website. These templates can be a valuable starting point for businesses developing their own policies https://www.sans.org/information-security-policy/
- **Incident Response Plan Template:** The Government of Canada provides a lot of free Cybersecurity resources, including this Incident Response Plan Template: https://ised-isde.canada.ca/site/cybersecure-canada/en/certification-tools/develop-incident-response-plan-fillable-template-and-example

www.ingramcontent.com/pod-product-compliance
Lightning Source LLC
LaVergne TN
LVHW022356060326
832902LV00022B/4480